UNPINNED

Also by Grant Watkins

CPR for Caregivers:
Connect, Project, & Reflect through Mind, Body, and Spirit

UNPINNED

Breaking the Hold of Sexual Assault and Abuse

Grant Watkins

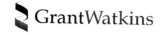

Tasora

Printed in the United States of America on acid-free paper.

ISBN 978-1-934690-33-8

Cover design by Kyle G. Hunter
Interior design by Rachel Holscher
Design, typesetting, and printing by BookMobile
Edited by Pat Samples and Mary Byers

To order additional copies of this book, please go to:
www.itascabooks.com

Author's note: The events described in these stories are real. Some places
and characters have fictitious names and identifying characteristics.

*It is so much easier to build strong children
than to repair broken men.*

FREDERICK DOUGLASS

Contents

Acknowledgments

There is a Zen proverb that says, "Leap and the net will appear." This was certainly the case when I decided to become responsible for my own recovery. When I made that leap, people appeared, almost magically, to create a net. These people surrounded me in support to aid me in my recovery and offered a platform from which my voice could be heard.

Thanks to the staff and volunteers of Neighborhood Involvement Program (N.I.P.) Minneapolis, Minnesota; Sexual Trauma and Assault Response Services (S.T.A.R.S.), a rape crisis center in El Paso, Texas; and Minnesota Circles of Support and Accountability (MNCOSA). My thanks to Dr. Karol Jensen, who asked me the hard questions; counselors John Bullough and Debby Gutierrez for guiding me through my journey; Ari Medina for helping me go public; and Detective Teresa Chavira for believing in me. Special thanks to my life partner and best friend, Matt Halley, for teaching me to love myself for who I am, and to fellow survivors and dear friends Lorrie Ramos and Gabrielle Hamen, who were there when I needed them to listen.

I will be forever grateful for the work that women and men all across this country have done to end sexual abuse and assault and to create social change. Their pioneering spirit has created a pathway for young boys and men like me to discover our own voice and the courage to speak out in the hope of healing others.

Introduction

"People never expect the obvious." So a widely respected El Paso businessman told me when I was in my early twenties. He was old enough to be my father and in many ways he was a mentor to me. I didn't think much of what he said at the time but in the two decades since, I have come to see the truth in it. It's easy to overlook the obvious when we trust people. When we do, sometimes the people we trust use their authority and power to abuse those who are vulnerable.

Like wrestlers, these abusers of power have great skill and knowledge and they're often revered. But those who revere them and trust them are taken by surprise when these power-seekers use their brute strength and willpower to pin down those around them physically, emotionally, spiritually, and sometimes even sexually. Even after an assault, if they're not successful in pinning down their victims, they will try to destroy them. For these brutal abusers, winning isn't about their skills and knowledge, it's about creating an illusion of power and control over those they abuse. In particular, if they can position themselves well politically and are regarded as pillars of the community, then the victims (those whom they have pinned) will be ridiculed by society, should they come forth with their stories of abuse.

Abusers who pin their victims often keep them in psychological captivity for years by making them and those around them believe that the abuse wasn't real. Over time, the abused stay pinned in an endless cycle of deception, unable to distinguish even for themselves the obvious. That's what happened to me.

I Have to Tell

Despite how humiliating and painful it is to tell my story, I am compelled to share it with others because I want many more people to become aware of the fact that boys and men are sexually assaulted. These boys and men need support when they come forward and begin the recovery process. I also want my story to motivate those who hear it to do whatever they can to prevent other males from being abused.

I believe most of the sexual assault that happens against boys and men goes unreported because we live in a world where the prevailing belief is that sexual assault only happens to women. This false idea alters our ability to "expect the obvious" despite how intelligent we may be. Most boys and men don't report the abuse because they don't fully realize what has happened to them. While it is commonly believed that sexual abuse of males is typically committed by gay men, the truth is that most of the abusers are heterosexual males whose choice of victim is not based on the victim's sexual orientation, ethnicity, age, or body size. Sexual assault is rarely about sex. It's usually about power and control.

I've often heard the statistic that one out of seven boys and one out of thirty-three men have been sexually abused. If left untreated, these individuals may experience life-threatening physical and psychological symptoms. Many of the survivors I've met are heterosexual, but I've also met several who are gay. Some of these men chose to cope with their abuse through sex, drug use, and alcohol addiction; others became chronically depressed and suicidal. I was lucky to survive the depression I experienced after being abused. Many men don't. According to SAVE.org, there are four male suicides for every female suicide, and more than 30,000 Americans die from suicide every year. Of course people kill themselves for a variety of reasons. I often considered suicide—and came close to killing myself—because of being abused. From my experience with these suicidal ideations and from what I've learned through the process of recovery, I suspect that many of the men who kill themselves were physically, sexually, or emotionally abused at one point in their lives, and felt like no one would be willing to listen to and believe their secrets. They directed their anger and hate toward themselves instead of at the people who abused them.

Time to Face the Abuser

After being sexual assaulted, part of me shut down. My spirit was broken and my heart was filled with fear. I was possessed by fear. I feared everyday things that reminded me of being attacked, ranging from relationships to hotel rooms, public bathrooms, soap, chain-link fences, and being alone. It was easier to stay home and feed my fear under the covers than to be out in the real world living up to my potential. I lived under the covers in fear for many years, until it was too painful to stay there anymore. There came a point when I knew that for me to get over the fear, I would have to face it, and that meant confronting the man who abused me.

You Too Can Recover

I'm OK now, but there was a time when I didn't think I was going to make it. Depression and suicidal ideations were symptomatic of the abuse I experienced as a child and young adult. If you've been abused and don't think you're going to make it, I want to assure you that you can, as long as you are willing to do the work. If you're feeling hopeless or suicidal, please contact your local suicide prevention hotline or rape crisis center immediately. Breaking the silence awakened the power within me and it can do the same for you. Eventually, the physical and emotional pain will lift and you will be whole again.

For years I kept the secret of my abuse to myself for fear that others might hate me, but the silence taught me to hate myself instead. Breaking the silence freed me from the pain even though it may have caused pain for others. Unpinning myself from the pain meant sharing my secret with others and getting angry at those who abused me. Learning to hate the abuse but to forgive the abuser was also part of unpinning myself, but forgiveness does not come overnight. For me, it was a process in which I learned to be gentle with myself and relied on the support of family, friends, and health care professionals who were willing to go with me and grow with me along the journey.

Self-Esteem Keeps Trying to Renew

The recovery process is different for everyone. For me it meant looking back at my childhood and the primary cause of my low self-esteem. Self-esteem is rooted in our childhood and despite how horrible our experiences may have been, our self–esteem is constantly trying to renew itself based on the support, warmth, and reassurance we receive from others. These renewing experiences with others help us restore our dignity and then empower us to go out and help others.

It took me years to figure out how to unpin myself and now I share those secrets with you. My heart no longer seeks to retaliate against my abuser but to help unpin others who have been abused sexually. If you are a survivor—male or female—know the pain that torments you can come to an end if you're willing to begin the journey.

The Truth Can Be Hard to Believe

The story you are about to read may seem unbelievable, but it's true. You may wonder how so much abuse could happen to one person. Let me assure you, it did happen and it happened to me. My experience of abuse at a young age severely damaged my sense of self-worth, placing me at higher risk of being further victimized. With low self-esteem, I looked to others for direction and failed to develop a sense of mastery over my environment, leaving me vulnerable to predators.

This is a story about moving from victim to survivor. Although my recovery process took place over a period of years, this book recounts my four-day journey to my childhood home, where I confronted my past and the man who raped me. The memories that were triggered along the journey helped me understand how my experiences growing up affected my self-esteem and my ability to recover from the rape. At times I was angry at God for not standing by me and making the pain go away faster. I realize now that it was my spirituality that supported me throughout the journey and unpinned me from the abuse that tormented me.

CHAPTER ONE

People Who Tell Disappear

One day in late March of 2006, I left the Catholic Basilica of Saint Mary in Minneapolis after meeting with my spiritual advisor. I sat in my car, pondering my next move. I had asked the Holy Spirit to take over and give me the strength to do what was necessary for my healing. After opening my eyes from prayer, I looked down and noticed my blue folder. This was the recovery folder I had carried around with me for the past two years. It was the same folder that, a few days later, I would leave on my bed for authorities to discover if I didn't make it back from El Paso. My inner voice said, *Go ahead, open it.*

I felt confident as I opened the folder. Inside it, next to my childhood photos, were papers filled with information I had collected from the Internet about the perpetrator—the Wrestler. I call the man who raped me the Wrestler because of the way he attacked me. He's not a professional wrestler, he's a prominent businessman, but somewhere in his life he must have learned the skills necessary to restrain his victims physically. On one of the sheets of paper in the folder was a business profile of my attacker that I had found posted on the website of the company where he worked.

As I sat in the car, thoughts continued to percolate in my mind about my plan to call him that day, in preparation for my El Paso trip. I looked up and saw the majestic basilica hovering over me as if it were offering me some sort of protection. My fingers slowly began to dial the number listed on the profile sheet. It was the number for the company's headquarters in El Paso, the city I had called home for the first thirty years of my life. As I was dialing, I began to think about the hours I had spent in therapy trying to find the courage to make this call and how he would respond. My hope was that an operator would answer and confirm that he still worked there. Instead I heard an automated answering system giving me the option of selecting from the company's staff directory. I quickly punched in his name and soon my call was being transferred. *Oh no,* I thought. Then my mind rested for a bit, realizing that I would probably get his voice mail since it was after hours.

When the ringing stopped, I was prepared to hang up quickly. But I did not get voice mail. I got the actual voice of the Wrestler! "Hello." *Oh my God, it's him. What should I do?* I hadn't heard this voice in almost two decades.

"This is Grant Watkins."

"Grant Watkins," he replied.

"Yes, Grant Watkins."

"Why, I haven't heard from you in . . . well, how long has it been? How are you? Didn't you move to Montana?"

"Well, up to the Midwest," I replied.

"Wow, it's been a long time. Well, what have you been up to?"

"I'm going to be visiting El Paso soon."

"Oh, well, what brings you back here?"

"You do."

"I do?" the Wrestler replied.

"Yes. I think it's time we have a talk."

"A talk. Well, we can have a talk here on the phone. What did you want to talk about?"

"Oh, you know." There was silence for a moment on both ends.

"I know."

"Yes, you know. We need to talk about what you did to me almost twenty years ago."

Another silent pause.

"OK," he replied. "Well, you don't need to come all the way down here for that."

"I do because of the way you hurt me."

"I hurt you?"

"Yes, you hurt me the night you raped me."

"I didn't rape you. We were just having fun. I know I was a bit rough with you and you said you didn't want to do that anymore, so we stopped. It was consensual."

"It was not consensual."

"Well, why are you calling me now after all these years? Why *now*? Is this like one of those church things that all of a sudden you remembered something? Were you a minor? Why now? Why after all these years? I saw you several times after that time, and you didn't mention anything about it. Why now?"

"How would you feel if someone raped one of your daughters?"

"That's not a problem. That's why they get married."

"That's why they get married!?" I replied. "That's really sick."

"What is it that you want? Is there some way we can work this out over the phone? You don't need to come all the way down here to heal. What do you want from me?"

"I want to talk to you face to face, eye to eye, man to man, and let you know what you did to me. You broke my spirit. You destroyed my young life."

"Why now after all these years?"

"Because I would rather face you while you're still alive than have to show up after you've died from old age. I don't want to stand on top of your grave reading my impact statement, spitting down on you."

"OK. OK. Fine. Fine. Where do you want to meet for coffee?"

"Oh no," I replied. "We're meeting with one of my advocates."

"One of your advocates? Who else have you told about this?"

"That's none of your business," I replied.

"Well, how do I know that this person has the right credentials?"

"Oh, she advocates for survivors of rape and sexual assault."

"Well, I don't think it's fair that you have someone there for you and I don't have someone with me."

"I don't think it's fair that you raped me. If you feel you need someone with you, then bring them. Bring your wife, your attorney. I don't really care. I just need to face you so that I can continue to heal."

"OK. OK. When?"

"I will fly in next Friday. My advocate will call you early in the morning to give you a place and time."

"Fine. Fine." He hung up the phone.

That phone call was one of the most profound steps I took toward my recovery. The process of reclaiming my life had begun.

Over the next few days I had lots of work to do. I needed to book my flight to El Paso, request time off from work, and notify Terri, a soft-spoken police detective in El Paso. I had been referred to Terri by the El Paso Police Department when I initially reported the assault several months earlier. It was a report that took me nearly twenty years to drum up the courage to make.

Once everything was in place, I had to tell my family, friends, and employer what I was going to do. In my heart I knew that I would be coming back, but just in case the Wrestler decided to hurt me, I wanted them to know where I was. I didn't tell anyone the exact date I would be leaving, however, because I didn't want anyone to try to stop me from going, or to go with me.

The fear of being murdered by the Wrestler had consumed me during my recovery. There was something about the way he looked at me right before he attacked and raped me. His eyes were hollow and filled with darkness as if some evil demonic spirit had come over him. His actions were much like a snake ready to devour its prey; he looked evil, although he remained silent as he began suffocating me.

For years I had nightmares of being attacked and I suppose you might even say I had become obsessed with feeling safe. I became paranoid about being attacked again or even murdered. The Wrestler once told me that to succeed in business you have to destroy the competition when they least expect it. Although I was not in business with the Wrestler, confronting him publicly meant exposing him and I knew it could impact his business relationships. I knew for certain he wouldn't think twice about destroying me. He had come very close to killing me once, and unless he had gotten professional help, he would be the same demonic man I had met twenty years earlier.

Standing Up for Myself

At age thirty, after ending a long-term relationship, I had decided to move to Minnesota to be closer to my family. The first few years were tough, but over time I grew to really enjoy the change in seasons and the new friendships I had developed. Yet depression and thoughts of suicide were commonplace for me. They normally surfaced when I heard about other people getting sexually assaulted or attacked. Certain smells, sounds, or the way someone touched me would trigger depression. Over the years, through therapy and other help, I had learned how to cope and to recognize that the feelings would eventually pass like a nasty thunderstorm rolling through a valley.

One morning, when I was forty, I woke up feeling paralyzed with fear. I didn't want to get out of bed and I didn't want to speak with anyone. There was a thickness in the air, everything seemed gloomy, and I began to consider ending my life. This time I knew the storm was not going to pass and I would not be able to go forward with my life unless I was willing to go back to the past and confront what had haunted me for a lifetime.

Some people have called me brave for making the journey back to confront the man who raped me. I never considered myself brave; I just wanted the hurt to go away. I thought that by standing up for myself, by confronting the Wrestler, I could somehow escape from the pain, anger, and grief that I felt. I often thought, *Who else has he inflicted pain on? Does he rape his wife, children, nieces, and nephews or does he prey on naive young men he meets? Young men like me, awkward and insecure. Perhaps he goes after boys who have not discovered a sense of themselves, looking outside themselves for approval and belongingness—those who are ignorant of the evils of the world.*

The senseless, evil deed of one man caused me years of emotional and physical pain. I was now at the final stage of claiming victory over my illness. Confronting the perpetrator would play an important role in helping me reestablish my self-esteem. Although I had physically survived the rape, years of silence had destroyed my self-image and that silence was slowly killing me.

It was time to confront the Wrestler, and I was willing to put my life in jeopardy to save it.

Going to El Paso

The time had come. My friend Heather sat in her car as it idled in the frigid April morning. My flight was to leave in just a few hours, and Heather was waiting to take me to the airport before starting her workday. I knew she was growing restless outside in her car, but I needed a few more minutes by myself inside my house. My house had been a place of refuge and healing as I journeyed through the recovery process. I walked through it one more time as if I were saying good-bye to all the things I had acquired in my lifetime. Passing my bedroom I stood in the doorway and said the prayer that had held me together for so many years, "Holy Spirit, guide me." I needed something greater than myself to lead the way. I didn't know what was waiting for me in El Paso, haunted as I was by a long-ago warning from the Wrestler, "People who tell disappear."

Although I had the support of the El Paso Police Department and knew that a therapist from the El Paso Rape Crisis Center would help facilitate the meeting, I still feared for my life. On my bed I left a few things for my family and the authorities to discover in case I didn't make it back. The most obvious was the suit I had chosen for my burial. It was solid black with a contrasting black stripe woven into its silklike material. Inside the suit jacket I had tucked a freshly pressed white shirt. I could feel the starch from the cleaners on my fingers as I unwrapped it from the plastic bag. Around the collar of the white shirt I placed a blue tie made of silk. Next to the suit was a pair of black socks and a pair of black shoes. I could still smell the fresh shoe polish I had used the night before to shine the shoes.

Next to my clothing was a copy of my will, burial request,

401(k) savings information, and enough money to bury me if my worst fear came true—an unfriendly, perhaps fatal, welcome to El Paso from the Wrestler. In a separate blue folder were notes about my recovery and detailed information about the man who had attacked me as a young man. I wanted the police to have everything on him—his name, photo, professional contacts, home and work addresses, political contribution information, and civic and volunteer activities.

My life had been filled with challenges, but what most filled my heart with anger and rage was the discovery that the Wrestler was still in a position of power and indirectly still working with youth. I knew I would not be in a position of power if I allowed my anger and rage to control me. For years these feelings were suppressed by depression and apathy, but over time I learned that whatever I was feeling was just part of the recovery process. Now, remaining calm and in control was what would give me the strength to do what I needed to do. Revenge was not my objective. My goals were to reclaim myself and to do my best to prevent him from striking again.

The Wrestler had said that what had happened between the two of us was consensual. I knew that there was nothing consensual about his attack. Confronting him would allow me to call it what it was—a brutal rape. I wanted to express how I felt, and I wanted him to know how the attack affected me. For the first time in years I could envision a path to feeling powerful and in control of my life. But the fear that had become ingrained in my being nagged me with questions. *What if he denied his actions and it caused me to have a relapse in my recovery? What if he retaliated against me? What if he found a way to publicly humiliate me by calling me a liar?*

In spite of my fears, I had made the decision that I, and all of humanity for that matter, would be better off if I confronted him. I would finally be set free of my depression and suicidal thoughts.

My hope was also that he would see himself as accountable for his actions and that the abuse of young people would stop.

I placed my suitcase in the back of Heather's car. There was no turning back, and I was about to break the silence that had bound me for so many years. Heather remained quiet as she drove me to the airport. That was fine; I didn't feel like talking. My mind was racing. *I'm on my way to confront the man who had taken so much from me. I need to confront him, man to man.* Brightly lit parking ramps and city streetlights illuminated the early morning sky as Heather and I approached the Minneapolis-St. Paul airport. My attention was drawn to the blinking Homeland Security Advisory sign outside the passenger drop-off area advising travelers about the level of threat to public safety. I wondered if the Department of Homeland Security would consider the Wrestler to be a threat to public safety. Although he had attacked me almost two decades earlier, I had lived most of my adult life feeling terrified, and I often wondered if he was still committing rape. Slowly we passed the advisory sign, and I had visions of a similar sign sitting in the Wrestler's front yard, warning his wife, family, and neighbors about his being a danger to their safety. The sign would only have one color code—red, indicating that he is likely to reoffend.

My fantasy of seeing the Wrestler publicly humiliated came to an abrupt halt as Heather pulled up to the curb and brought her car to a complete stop. We looked at each other, not knowing what to say. I could see the fear in her eyes, and I'm sure she could sense my insecurity about whether I'd make the trip back home. After hugs and a few words of good-bye, I found myself standing on the curb outside the airline's check-in desk, suitcase and backpack in hand.

The sun was beginning to rise and wake up the rest of Minneapolis, and I realized that my flight would not depart until 11:15 a.m., leaving me with a few hours to reflect. It dawned on me that I might have been better off sleeping in and taking a cab to the airport than arranging for a ride from Heather at the crack of dawn.

After checking in and finding my departure gate, I paced back and forth for hours. Too tired to read and too excited to sit still, I felt my heart racing. So much was at stake for me. Finally, I heard a voice announce that boarding was about to begin. I immediately moved toward the door and stood in line to have my boarding pass checked. After I made my way down the narrow path to my seat, I sat down and sighed a deep breath of relief. *I made it. Nothing can stop me now.* I then began to reflect on the series of events that triggered my epiphany about being raped and other experiences of being sexually assaulted.

I opened my backpack and pulled out a folder that held a picture of me as a child. In the photo sits a four- or five-year-old kid with sandy blond hair and big brown eyes. He smiles halfheartedly, as if wondering whether he will ever feel safe. My eyes filled with tears as I held it. Not only was I standing up for myself as an adult, but for the very first time I was standing up for this boy. As a child, I had been stepped on in many ways and abandoned by some of those responsible for caring for me. That wounded, frightened child lived on in me into adulthood, unable to cope with the assaults on his body and mind. Integrating a connection between my mature, recovering adult self and my inner child would be crucial to how I would live out the rest of my life.

As a child, I felt emotionally castrated by my father and older brother. My father was a tall man, with olive skin, dark hair, and green eyes. He had an athletic build and masculine facial features, much like my brother, who also had dark hair and similar

skin color. Any chance of having a normal boyhood and growing into manhood was thwarted by the emotional detachment
I felt from my father and the physical abuse I experienced from
my older brother in the early years of my life. When most children are establishing their sense of self-worth, mine was being
ripped in half by the males in our family. In my recovery, I've
worked hard at living in the now, the present moment, but I
often think this emphasis on present-moment living is over-
rated by New Age gurus. It is our past that gives creation to the
present moment and sometimes we have to look back to figure
out how to free ourselves from the emotional stronghold that
is pinning us down and preventing us from living our lives to
their fullest potential.

I can remember when I was a child peering into a big box of
family photos taken before I was born. My mother looked like
Snow White. She had wavy black/brownish hair and very light
skin. Mom's bone structure was much smaller than my dad's,
and her facial features were much softer, much like mine. In the
same box was a photo of a naked infant sleeping on my father's
chest. The photo was not of me, it was of my brother five years
before I was born. For me, the photo affirmed the deep bond
that he had with Dad. It was a bond that I didn't think I would
ever experience.

My father adored his firstborn son. Dad often referred to
him as "Captain K" or his "number one son." I was painfully
aware of being number two. I begged for any attention I could
get from my father, but the bond between Dad and Captain K
did not leave space for me. As a toddler I would pull at my father's pants in hopes of him picking me up and giving me some
sort of attention. Pushing me toward my mother, he wanted
nothing to do with me. I was the product of a failed vasectomy,
a medical mishap. In retrospect I suppose any man willing to
put his testicles under a knife must be serious about preventing

an unwanted pregnancy and would find it difficult to love something he tried so hard to prevent.

I grew up thinking my father was not at the hospital the day of my birth. I once heard he dropped Mom off at the hospital and went out of town to a coaching camp. Coaching camp, fishing expedition, or visiting the man in the moon, it doesn't really matter. Whether he was there or not, as a child I could sense my father's disappointment in me and felt his resentment.

I may have been a mistake, but Captain K's birth was a celebration that would be recognized for years to come. It wasn't until Captain K's tenth birthday that his paradise began to shatter. Our parents filed for divorce around that time and as a sixth grader Captain K became the man of the house. He resented being in that position. Captain K was more prepared for the divorce than I and my other two siblings were, though. He received a special kind of nurturance that firstborns often do. This nurturing gave him a sense of self-worth that I was denied. As an adult, he would probably argue that his belief in himself came from his relationship with Jesus Christ, but I believe the seeds of his high self-esteem were planted long before he knew anything about Jesus. It was apparent early on that he felt the love of both Mom and Dad, where I only felt cared for by my mother.

Although Captain K resented my parents' divorce and his added responsibilities of helping Mom out, I think in his mind he enjoyed being the little man of the house, king of the castle, and master of all. He had complete dominion over me and ruled with an iron fist. Although I feared him I also revered him as my older brother, as odd as that might sound. Because I witnessed my father beating my mother, I wanted to protect her and I grew closer to her, whereas Captain K grew closer to my father. Perhaps his being close to Dad is how he learned to be emotionally and physically violent. Despite our parents' separation the bond between Dad and Captain K continued to grow.

Dad taught football and track, and the two of them spent hours together watching and participating in many sporting events. Captain K wanted to play sports with me too, but instead of throwing the ball *to* me he normally threw the ball *at* me so that it landed in the center of my face or upside my head. Early on I grew to fear sports.

In addition to my father teaching Captain K about sports, the two of them spent many hours on hunting and fishing trips. I was left at home with my mother. I don't recall ever wanting to go fishing or hunting, but I do recall wanting to bond with my older brother and Dad and could not understand why they hated me so much. Was it because I looked more like my mother than my father? Did Captain K see me as a threat to his relationship with our father? Did the two of them sense that I was different from most boys my age?

As children, there is one thing my siblings and I did have in common and that was a deep religious faith. We had learned it from our mother, who had accepted Jesus Christ as her personal lord and savior as a little girl. Perhaps going to church several times a week is what kept my mother sane during her childhood and her early years of marriage to my father. Even Dad professed his faith in Christ after my parents' divorce. I'm not so sure he really believed in Christ or if he was just calling out for help because his life was upside down and he didn't know where else to turn. My own belief in Jesus Christ caused me more pain than joy.

It's much easier to love yourself if you think God loves you. However, what I was taught as a child was that God doesn't love people who are "different," and that's how I felt. I didn't have any way as a child to name what might be causing that feeling; I just knew that in some way I wasn't "normal." That was distressing to me. The certainty that God didn't love me made it much harder for me to love myself. I also came to believe at a very early age that only "normal" people are going to heaven and everyone else is going to hell to live with snakes for eternity. I didn't have much to look forward to. Growing up in the church I did had a big impact on my sense of self-worth. I suspect that the types of teachings I heard there have cost many young people their lives through suicide when they felt unworthy of being alive.

2

My thoughts were interrupted when the pilot instructed the flight attendants to prepare for landing. My mouth got dry, which it often does when I'm nervous. My hands were shaking and I felt agitated. I was excited to confront my attacker but nervous as hell. *What was the Wrestler thinking? Would I be going back to Minnesota alive?*

As the tires hit the runway in El Paso, I felt sick to my stomach. Once the plane came to a complete stop, I took a deep breath, gathered my things from under the seat in front of me, and made my way down the aisle.

CHAPTER TWO

Day 1

Arrival in El Paso, Wednesday, April 5, 2006

When the airplane door opened, I did my best to walk out confidently, staying alert for anyone around me who might look suspicious. Although I arrived two days before my scheduled appointment with the Wrestler, I worried that anytime during my stay in El Paso my life could be in danger.

El Paso is on the Mexican border next to Juárez, and I had learned through reading the *El Paso Times* online that Juárez had become one of the most dangerous places on earth because of Mexican drug cartels. I had no reason to believe that the Wrestler was involved with any illegal drug activity, but I had heard he was well connected on both sides of the border, and I thought he might see me as a threat should my accusations of his raping me become public.

I walked out into the airport and things did not look very familiar. Over time the airport had been renovated and was not the same airport I grew up with. After gathering my luggage, I walked outside and basked in the Texas sun.

As I stretched my arms and legs, I felt glorious. Living in

Minnesota I had not seen blue skies or felt much warmth from the direct sun in months. Suddenly my heart began to race when I realized that the Wrestler might be waiting for me outside. *What if he tries to shoot me in front of the airport? What if he hired someone to knock me off? I know he agreed to meet with me, but there was reluctance in his voice.* I quickly went back inside and called for transportation to take me over to the car rental area. I didn't want to be seen as open prey for a would-be attacker. If someone was following me, I didn't want this person to know where I was or what I would be doing next.

Once I picked up my rental car, I drove around for a while, making sure no one was following me. There were several things I wanted to do before the end of the day. I wanted to begin visiting the people and places that had shaped me in my youth and to confront those that had left scars on my psyche. I first drove over to Griggs Restaurant, just a few miles east of the airport, where I would begin to catch up with old friends.

Griggs Restaurant

I had grown up working in the restaurant and was very fond of the owners. I had met them when I was in elementary school. I had a childhood crush on their daughter and eventually went to work at the restaurant when I was in junior high. My first real job was making corn tortillas, not a job I enjoyed very much. Though making tortillas is a simple process, it's a tough job. Once you make the masa, which consists of corn flour and water, you place it on a conveyer belt that moves it through an industrial stove.

I don't recall much else about making tortillas other than that the room gets really hot and your hands burn as you pick the tortillas off the grill. Thank God for cross training. I was grateful to take a break from tortilla making to wash dishes and bus tables. Eventually I moved up the ladder and worked in the front of the restaurant and helped with the daily operations.

The close relationship I had with Griggs and the Duke family started when I was in my teens and lasted into my midtwenties. I thought Mr. Duke looked like Elvis, but with silvery white hair, bushy sideburns, and a big belly. He always wore cowboy boots and Western pants that looked like they were made of polyester material. He was very personable and was a great role model for me. Mr. Duke taught me valuable lessons in life about hard work, ethics, and integrity. Sometimes, though, I would find him not telling Mrs. Duke the truth about what he was eating. She always seemed to be concerned about his weight and I would often find him hiding in the walk-in refrigerator snacking on food he wasn't supposed to eat.

Mrs. Duke had blond hair and pretty facial features just like my mother. She was also in great shape and seemed to enjoy life. I learned my first lesson in gossip when I went to Mrs. Duke and told her some rumors I had heard about a schoolmate. She gently looked at me and said, "Grant, I think that might be gossip and that's not something you want to be known for." She looked me in the eye and smiled to let me know that she still liked me but didn't approve of my gossiping. After that day I always thought twice before spreading rumors about others.

What I most admired about Mrs. Duke was her ability to cut to the chase. If she didn't believe what a person was telling her, she would roll her eyes and then grin, looking directly back at the person without saying another word. I got the impression that Mr. Duke was good at telling tall tales, and Mrs. Duke spent a lot of time cutting through the bull.

My relationship with Mr. Duke at times was very difficult, like riding a roller coaster. He had a quick temper but always came back validating me with a strong affirmation. He went out of his way to support me in many of my endeavors. In some ways he filled a father figure role for me. One of the most important things that I remember about Mr. Duke was the way he taught me how to drive a stick shift. He had an old white pickup that we used for running supplies back and forth between his two restaurants. After I got my driver's license, one morning he asked me to take some supplies to the west side of town. Mr. Duke and I walked out to the truck and he threw me the keys. I told him I didn't know how to drive a stick shift and he told me not to worry, that he was going to teach me. Boy, do I remember how nervous I was to drive his truck. I started the engine, put the truck in first gear, and began to drive. The engine stalled. For the life of me I could not coordinate shifting the gears. I felt frustrated and wanted to give up. After a few moments, Mr. Duke asked me to shut off the truck. He then went on to explain that driving shift is just like dating a girl. Your moves have to be coordinated. If you push too fast, you'll scare her away. If you move too slow, she'll lose interest. The rhythm is everything.

I was a clumsy, naive teenager and I was thinking he was really trying to tell me about the birds and the bees. Nonetheless, that day I learned how to drive a stick shift. Once I was able to get this concept in my head, I started the truck again and away we went, fast and furious, down Montana Avenue.

I think it was one of the most enjoyable rides I have ever taken. I learned the art of driving shift, but I also learned the art of working with people. It's all in the rhythm of things. If we push too hard on a friendship, then we can choke it. If we move too slow, then we give the impression to others that we don't really care.

The second most important thing I remember about this man was the love he had for his wife and kids. Growing up, I had a crush on his daughter Shawn. I first noticed this feeling in the second or third grade when she invited me to sit with her at lunch. Shawn looked more like her dad than she did her mother and she was also a bit bossy. I liked her bossiness. She came across as very confident, a quality I had very little of. She never made me feel bad for not being the smartest boy in class. I think Shawn was smarter than I was and I know for sure she could color much faster and still stay in the lines.

One day in the second grade, our teacher, Mrs. Beissel, asked us to recite the alphabet. When the letter Q came up Shawn yelled out. "That's my mother's name, Q." Some of the kids began to snicker when Mrs. Beissel asked Shawn how her mother spells her name. Shawn replied, "Just like you see it in the alphabet— Q." This struck me as being something really serious. I thought Shawn's mother must be very important if the people who made the alphabet decided to name a letter after her.

My feelings for Shawn continued to grow stronger although at the same time I knew there was something different about me that would not make for marriage material, even if I wasn't sure what it was. I just knew I was different.

Shawn and I grew up in the same church and attended the same school for most of our childhood and youth. In high school Shawn transferred to Hanks High School and I escorted her to a dance. I don't recall if it was her prom or a homecoming dance. There was nothing in this world more important to Mr. Duke than his kids, and he wanted this event to be something very special for his daughter. I think he also knew more about me at the time than I knew about myself and he felt safe letting his daughter go on a date with me.

Mr. Duke and I sat down and talked about all of the expenses related to the dance. I told him that I didn't have much money and could barely afford to rent the tuxedo for the dance. Mr. Duke made sure I had enough money to cover all my expenses and then rented a sports car for me to drive the night of the dance. He even allowed me to keep the car for the entire weekend. On the day of the dance, Mr. Duke took me to a restaurant that was located on top of one of the buildings in downtown El Paso. He showed me where to park my car, introduced me to the maître d', and then reviewed the dinner menu with me so I wouldn't be at a total loss later that evening. I know Mr. Duke did this more for his daughter than he did for me, but nonetheless I found this time with Mr. Duke to be very special. After the dance, I did something I had wanted to do for a long time and that was to kiss Shawn. From what I remember it didn't go as planned and I ended up kissing her on the cheek instead of the lips. I drove away from her house that night feeling both confused about my sexuality and frustrated that I didn't have the confidence to be more assertive with Shawn.

As I grew older, I realized that God had other plans for me than falling in love with a woman and getting married. Nonetheless, I still had strong feelings for Shawn, and somewhere in the back of my mind I thought I would marry her and help run the family business. Fortunately for both of us, that never happened. She went away to college and fell in love with another young man. On the day of that wedding I was sitting in the Griggs office with Mr. Duke when I suddenly realized that I would not be part of this family. I felt sad—hurt even—and I was about to cry when Mr. Duke asked me what I was doing. I turned to him and said, "Just thinking." He snapped back, "Well, go think on your own time, not mine." I got up from the desk and left the room without saying a word. It was just too painful to stay there. That evening I went to the wedding and stood in the back of the church with my mother and sister. A man from the church we grew up in turned to me and said, "Shouldn't that be you up there?" I broke down crying, realizing that was never going to be.

A few friends from the restaurant told me Shawn never had the same feelings for me that I had for her. I understood but that didn't make my pain go away. At the wedding I think I was grieving for more than just a lost love. I was also grieving the fact that I wasn't like most other men.

It had been years since I had been in the restaurant, so when I got out of the rental car and walked in, things seemed a little surreal. Chris, one of the waitresses, was the only person I knew who was still working at the restaurant. I looked around for other familiar faces, but there were none. In my mind I saw the image of one of the floor managers. He was a Hispanic man who used to call me Señorito. At the time I thought that was a compliment, but later learned it was a derogatory term, like "faggot."

Then I thought back to another Griggs experience that left me feeling inadequate. I was in my early twenties and working in the front when one of my high school buddies came in with his family. We had both worked there as teenagers. My friend, who was home from college, looked at me and asked me when I was going to get a real job. To me this *was* a real job—I enjoyed working at the restaurant. I should have told my friend to f— off, but I didn't. I just got mad and I was also a little jealous. As he sat at a table with his dad, I was resentful that he had never had to spend a day as a caregiver for either of his parents, while I had spent many months being a caregiver for my dad when he became ill. My friend also didn't have to work and his parents were paying all of his college and living expenses. Meanwhile I was trying to put myself through college not only working a full-time job but also working at Griggs on a part-time basis.

When my friend sat down with his family, all I wanted to do was pour salsa on him.

It wasn't too long after seeing him in the restaurant that my time working at Griggs came to an end. I did my best to stay in touch with Mr. Duke. I always made it a point to call him on his birthday. When I was in Europe, I sent him a postcard. When I returned home from that trip, my mother called and told me Mr. Duke had passed away.

I did not feel too bad about missing the funeral because I knew that Mr. Duke didn't like funerals anyway. When my father died, only Mrs. Duke and her mother came to the funeral. Later, when I asked Mr. Duke why he didn't come to Dad's funeral, he got choked up and said that he didn't like funerals because "death is final and I don't like the feeling of not being able to do something about it." I think Mr. Duke knew that he couldn't change me either, although I'm sure he wanted too. Mr. Duke knew about the relationship I had with my father. Sometime after the funeral I do recall him saying to me, "You lost something you never had, son—a dad." Over the years I got the sense that the Dukes meant more to me than I meant to them. I'm sure Mr. and Mrs. Duke were parenting lots of young kids as they found their first employment in their family-run restaurant. I guess it doesn't really matter how the Dukes felt about me. I'm just grateful to have been nurtured by them at a time that was important to me.

As I sat at the table in Griggs fondly recalling these experiences with the Dukes, Chris served me a glass of iced tea and then brought me a green chicken enchilada with sour cream. It was one of my favorite dishes at Griggs. We chatted for a while and I told her why I was in town. Since I had not met with the Wrestler yet and was still concerned about my safety, I asked her not to tell anyone about my being in El Paso until I was back on a plane to Minnesota.

Cielo Vista Elementary School

After leaving Griggs I drove over to Cielo Vista Elementary School, which I attended as a child. I needed to confront something that had happened to me when I was in the first or second grade. I'm not sure which grade I was in, since I repeated the first grade and the timeline is a bit fuzzy to me now. I was not a very bright kid. Sitting still and staying focused were challenges for me, as were reading, writing, and math. In the early 1970s there was little understanding of ADD and dyslexia. These diagnoses were not assigned to me until much later in life. All I knew was that it took me longer than other kids took to figure things out. Going back to Cielo Vista brought back many memories of feeling inferior.

It was late in the school day when I drove up to the one-story redbrick building. I didn't think it would look good if a man from out of state showed up in a rental car and started walking the halls of the school, so I parked nearby in front of the home of Mrs. Miller, who had been a teacher at the school when I went there.

The first thing that caught my eye as I looked at the school was the chain-link fence that surrounded the school yard on the north side of the building. The fence reminded me of a time when I was playing on the playground with some schoolmates. It was a new school year and I didn't know many of the kids. Since I was new to their class, the kids formed a circle around me, holding hands. They all began to skip and run, keeping me in the center of the circle. Everyone was laughing and having a good time and I felt very special in that moment. The kids were chanting my name when some other kids, from the class I was in the year before, approached us. One of these kids recognized me from the year before and told everybody that my name was Flunker. "Flunker, Flunker," he called out. Suddenly my laughter turned to horror as my new friends started calling me Flunker. I started to yell back, "My name is Grant!"

By this time several classes of kids were out on the playground. One of my older sisters said to the kids around me, "His name isn't Grant, it's Grunt." Grunt is a name Captain K had been calling me at home. That name was now following me back to school and the humiliation only got worse. I was stunned and embarrassed. Some kids were calling me Flunker and other kids were calling me Grunt. In my attempt to run from the name callers, I ran to the gate of the chain-link fence, but I was unable to open it, and I felt trapped. That is the earliest memory I have of wishing I were dead.

Once all the school buses and parents had picked up the kids, I entered the front doors of the school and headed for the office. I asked the person behind the front desk if I could speak with the principal. She told me that the principal was in a meeting. My throat began to tighten as I told this woman that I wanted to go into the boys' bathroom so I could confront something about my past. I was doing everything I could to keep from crying as I began to tell her what had happened to me as a young child. The woman looked like she was going to get a bit teary-eyed too. She suddenly cut me off and said, "Let me find someone who can help you."

A small-framed mature woman soon greeted me at the desk. She was the assistant principal. My voice still cracking, I began telling her that I attended the school as a young child and was sexually violated as a little boy. Part of my healing meant going back into the bathroom to see where this had happened. I sensed that the assistant principal was also a bit shaken by what I was telling her as we walked down the hall. When we arrived at the boys' bathroom, she walked inside to make sure it was all clear. There was no one in there, and she told me to take as much time as I needed.

As I pushed open the wooden door, I thought I was going to break down emotionally, but I didn't. I looked over at the small urinal on the wall where I was first confronted by the perpetrators. I walked over to the urinal and then turned around and looked at the toilet and bathroom stall where I had been held captive. I stood in the same place where the boys who attacked me had stood.

I only stayed in the bathroom for a short time. There was no pain or anger, just relief that this memory could no longer hurt me anymore. As an adult I had spent hours crying over the loss of my innocence; I guess there were just no tears left in me. When I walked out of the bathroom, the assistant principal was waiting for me. She listened as I finished telling her my story.

Karl and I were skipping rocks across the playground when Karl called some older boys sissies. The boys were older than us, perhaps eight or ten years older. I assumed they were from the local junior high or high school. One of them was quite fat. The boys began to chase Karl, but he outran them and eventually got away. Karl was known for inciting conflict with other kids and then leaving his friends to handle the turmoil that ensued. But this time it was different, very different. I was about to experience the long-term consequences of Karl's deviant behavior. What he did left a deep scar in my psyche that would contribute to my feeling insecure for years to come.

When the older boys took off after Karl, I went into the school to use the bathroom before I left for home. I walked past school faculty who were finishing up their day's work and past the janitor, who was sweeping the long hallway by the lockers. I remember entering the bathroom and smelling the pink hand soap and an astringent cleaner that smelled like Comet. To this day, when I smell Comet or feel its gritty sandiness, the sensation triggers emotions in me that take me back to that afternoon.

After peeing, I heard the older boys who had been chasing Karl enter the bathroom. I turned around and the fat boy started yelling at me that he was not a girl. He then began to unzip his pants and lift his shirt, exposing his genitals to me. When he lifted up his shirt, I could see layers of fat and his chest looked like he had little breasts. His face and skin color were milky white and he had thick curly brown hair. From a distance he really did look like a fat teenage girl.

I think I went into a state of shock when I saw his penis. At first I thought it was a joke. His penis was different from mine and much bigger but what really confused me was his pubic hair. I had never seen pubic hair and I thought that somehow he had a wig inside his pants. I couldn't make sense of what was going on, much less defend myself. I was afraid he was going to beat me up like Captain K often did.

I began to scream as the boy got closer to me. I tried running from him but I couldn't get away. Each time he blocked me with his body and continued exposing his genitals. Sometimes I still feel uneasy when I think about it. What puzzles me most is that the depth of emotional pain I have felt doesn't seem to match up with the images of what I recall happening. I do recall him restraining me but I can't recall if he forced me to engage in a sexual act with him or if he just intimidated me by exposing himself. You would think that I could easily recall something like that, but I don't and when I force myself to reflect deeper about it, I begin to feel nauseous and terror overcomes me. For now I have decided to let it go, because I know the mind is powerful and it will reveal further details when I'm emotionally, physically, and spiritually ready to handle them. I have little recollection of the boy who was with him. I do remember that he was holding the door to the bathroom closed and wouldn't let me out, so I kept running around in circles. It appeared as if he didn't fully understand what was going on.

In my attempt to get away from the boy who was exposing himself to me, I ran into a bathroom stall but he came in after me. My body was shaking and I was screaming and crying for help as loud as I could. At some point I heard the other boy yell at his friend to leave me alone. He then said something about leaving and not wanting to be part of what was happening. The fat boy backed away but then made some type of threat toward me. I'm not sure if he was threatening me because he thought I was the one who called him a sissy or if he was threatening me to keep me from telling anyone about what he had done to me in the bathroom.

I don't recall whether the two boys left the bathroom first, or if I did, but I have a faint memory of breaking loose from the fat boy and running under the arms of his friend as he held the door, trying to exit himself.

Once I escaped from the bathroom, I ran toward the front entrance of the school, but the older boys must have run past me because I remember seeing them in front of the school waiting for me to come out. I stopped and turned around and saw Captain K and his friend Paul standing at the opposite end of the corridor from where I was standing. I started to walk toward Captain K and his friend to tell them what had happened. Before I could speak, Captain K grabbed a homework assignment I was carrying from me. He ripped it into pieces and threw it in a nearby trash can.

Meanwhile I could see the older boys who had just physically and sexually intimidated me walking out by the flagpole. I tried telling Captain K about the incident, but he wouldn't listen. He just kept chastising me about the paper and the grade I had made on it. When I started to cry, he said he was going to tell my mother.

Tell my mother what? I wondered. *That I had just been attacked by some older boys or that he tore up a homework assignment I had in my hand?* Captain K continued to try impressing his friend Paul by pushing me around and mocking me, and then walked away laughing. As I walked home crying I wondered what to do about the horrible feelings churning inside me. I wanted to tell my mom what had happened, but Captain K told me to stop crying or he was going to tell my mom. I concluded that I would get in trouble if she found out, so I didn't bring it up again until I was much older.

Although I did not tell the assistant principal the story in detail, I felt her concern about what had happened to me. She was on her way to a study hall for unruly kids and she asked if I would like to join her. At first I was a bit hesitant, but I agreed. We entered the same classroom where I used to attend math with Mrs. Smith. It seemed kind of funny because the chairs and tables were so small. I sat down in a circle next to a few kids and the assistant principal. Something about meeting the little kids transformed the way I was viewing my own childhood sexual assault. I stopped thinking of the older boys as violent attackers. I came to understand the incident as boys trying to prove their manhood. On that day, with the help of a very wise assistant principal, I walked away from that school leaving some of my pain behind.

Shaver Street and My Mother

After leaving the school I drove through my neighborhood to the house I grew up in on Shaver Street. The new owners had added a covered porch, new roof, fresh paint, and a new landscape. The changes looked great and I couldn't help but wonder what changes they had made on the inside of the house. When our family lived there, Mom was constantly making changes on the interior and exterior. Having a nice house and nice things boosted her sense of self-worth.

My mother must have needed this boost because of the many difficulties she experienced while growing up and also while she was married to my father. Yet, in many ways, she seemed to have a strong sense of herself. Mom was guided by strong principles, many of them coming from the teachings she had learned from the Christian church of her youth. She tried to instill these principles in her children, and though I no longer agree with her on many of the things she taught me about God, Jesus, and religion, I do value the principles of honesty and integrity I learned from her.

I remember particularly well one lesson she taught me about honesty. Sometime after moving into our house on Shaver Street, we went to the funeral of a great-aunt whom I had never met. My mother, grandmother, and two aunts, along with several cousins, met somewhere between Monahans and Midland, Texas, in order to travel together the many miles to where the funeral was being held.

Money was tight back then, so all of us (four adults and seven children) shared one motel room with two double beds. The adults got the beds and all the kids nestled into sleeping bags on the floor.

The following morning I noticed my mom reading the sign on the back of the motel room door. This sign explained the additional charges for extra people sleeping in the room. My mother then began to count out her money on the end of the bed. My aunt asked her what she was doing and she told her she was coming up with the additional money to pay for the extra people in the room.

I remember my mother receiving quite a bit of criticism from the other adults for paying the extra money. During a debate about the topic among all of the women in the room, one of my aunts yelled out, "If you pay the extra money, we will have no money to buy the kids ice cream later today." Then we kids started in on my mom about spending the extra money on the motel room and we did our best to prevent her from paying it. Everyone was upset with my mother, but she took a stand for honesty. Mom paid the money to the motel and all the kids stayed angry with her for spending "our" ice cream money. I realize now that the ice cream would have come and gone but the lesson in integrity will live on forever.

The other thing that lives on in my mind about my great-aunt's funeral was the ride over to the funeral home. After checking out of the motel we asked for directions to the funeral home. The motel clerk gave us directions, but we soon found ourselves lost in the small community where the funeral was going to take place.

Mom was driving our big yellow station wagon and the car was packed tight with my grandmother, aunts, cousins, and sisters. It was hot that day and the windows were all down. We drove through the small west Texas town, passing small shops and entering a residential neighborhood. At some point we stopped seeing houses and found ourselves at a dead end street. Mom stopped the car abruptly when the street we were driving on suddenly came to an end, which got everyone's attention. One aunt said, "Turn the car around." Then someone said, "Look for a street sign," but there were none. All we could see were dirt hills with lots of open land. Mom turned the car around and we drove a little farther before the street suddenly stopped again.

The tension in the car started to rise as the adults tried to figure out where we were. Far off in the distance we could see some metal buildings that had no windows. In front of one of the buildings was a man in a white truck waving a flag at us. About the same time, we heard the roar of an engine close by, but when we looked all around us, we did not see anyone else on the street.

Then one of the kids pointed up in the sky and we saw a very small plane flying over our yellow station wagon. By this time the man in the white truck had driven closer to our car. He was furiously waving his flag and making hand gestures for us to follow him. Mom, along with the other adults, finally came to the realization that we had gotten lost on the runway of the community airport. Once we got off the runway, everyone in the car started to laugh and I felt a sense of belonging and the love of my family.

Crybaby, Crybaby

The first memory I have of my mother is an experience in my infancy that also involved Captain K:

The dampness of my diaper awakens me from my afternoon nap. Or is it the deviant behavior of my older brother? My cry is the only language I have to express my need for my mother. Before my mother arrives, my brother, who is five years older than I, stands beside my crib. I am happy to see him. My arms reach up for him to hold me.

He does not have the height or strength to lift me out of the crib, so I begin to reach out to him. His hands reach out to mine and he begins pulling my infant body tight against the railing. It hurts. Gripping my hands and arms, he begins to pull tighter and tighter. Each time he pulls, my cry becomes louder and louder. I do not feel safe. My body shakes with fear.

Suddenly my mother appears. Captain K releases his snakelike grip, and the pain begins to subside. My mother picks me up and gently holds me close to her. I feel safe again. Captain K gives Mom a look of innocence and darts out of the room.

This incident was the first in a series of abusive experiences I remember from my childhood and early adulthood that, together, almost destroyed me. When I began the hard work of recovery, I wanted very badly to heal from them, but I did not think anyone would believe that all those things had happened to me. Doing the work of healing was very painful. I constantly asked myself how one person could experience so much abuse in his lifetime while some people never have the experience of being taken advantage of. I soon realized that having low self-esteem from childhood played a significant role in attracting my perpetrators. Perpetrators prey on weak people.

As I continued the work of healing, more and more I kept asking myself where my self-confidence was. *How come I have none? What happened to me?* Over time I started to have flashbacks of my older brother attacking me just like the Wrestler had done but the attacks were not sexual in nature, just violently physical. I learned to be a victim early in life when I didn't have the physical or emotional strength to defend myself. Since most of the physical abuse I experienced from my brother happened behind my parents' backs, there was no intervention from a caring adult. I did not learn how to thrive or even how to survive with much sense of self-worth. It was not until I became an adult that I became aware of what happened early on in my life and unlearned my identity as a victim.

There were times Captain K would wrestle me to the ground and then sit on my face and fart into my mouth and nostrils. His favorite head game was to fart in to a glass and then tip the glass onto the carpet. When I would pass him walking through the den he would grab onto my leg and wrestle my small-framed body to the ground while pulling my face near to the upside-down glass. Then he would slowly lift the glass, making me inhale his toxic farts. One day he wrestled me to the ground and then called my older sister into the room to finish me off. He held me down as she sat on my stomach and began pounding on my face and upper body as he cheered her on. She did everything my older brother told her to do. I've never understood why she allowed him to have so much control over her childhood. Perhaps on some level she lived in fear of standing up for herself and knew that if she didn't beat on me, she herself would have been beaten by Captain K. Having my sister and brother beat me like that was humiliating and made me feel like I was going insane.

Once I was able to get up off the floor, I ran out the front door and jumped on my bike. I didn't want to go back home to that kind of abuse. My shoestrings were untied and they were getting caught in the spokes. I remember thinking that I wanted to die and was hoping my loose shoestrings would get caught in the chain and cause the bike to crash, killing me. When that didn't happen, I closed my eyes and drove my bike through a stop sign, hoping that a car would hit me and I would die. At the time I didn't know what the word suicide meant. All I knew was that I didn't want to be with my older brother anymore and I was certain that my older brother wanted nothing to do with me. He was continually attacking me, physically or verbally, but at the time I wasn't aware that what was happening to me was abuse. I only knew that being wrestled by my older brother and taunted hurt like hell and it always seemed to happen when my parents were not around.

When I was in the fourth grade, I told Mrs. Dominquez, my Spanish teacher, to call me Mama's Boy. She looked at me surprised and asked me who was calling me a mama's boy. I told her my older brother called me that, along with a bunch of other names. She told me I should tell my parents about this, but I had learned a long time ago not to tell my parents anything unless I wanted to get the shit beaten out of me. If I complained about Captain K to my parents they would get mad at him and he would get back at me. It was a vicious circle, so I learned at an early age to stay out of the house as much as possible.

2

I spent a lot of time at my best friend Joey's house. It seemed safe there, and I was far away from Captain K. Joey's dad never pushed me away like my dad did and on one occasion I remember his parents adding me to their gym membership. On Saturday nights we would go to Mass. Joey's parents, Joe and Juanita, were Catholic and my family was Baptist. The fact that I was attending their church didn't go over well with my parents, but I continued to go anyway. I felt safe in their church and I don't recall it having as many rules as the Baptist church. Plus it got me out of the house and far away from Captain K.

The physical abuse from my older brother continued into my early teens. My parents built a swimming pool and I learned that if Captain K was swimming in the pool, I'd better stay out. If I entered the pool, Captain K would come up on me like a shark and pull me to the bottom of the pool. I hated it when he submerged my head under water for long periods of time. I felt like I was drowning. It wasn't just horseplay. These were violent attacks, and there was no way I could defend myself.

Captain K went off to college, where he learned how to rope cattle and chew tobacco. When he came home I remember one day walking by him on the sidewalk in front of our home. He threw his rope around me, pulled me down to the ground, and dragged me up the sidewalk. He and his friend then sat back and laughed.

The most painful memory of my older brother is around the same time, when he tackled me in my bedroom. My back was against the carpet and my arms extended on the floor behind my head. As he was holding down my arms, he squatted over me and dribbled tobacco juice onto my face. I remember clenching my lips tightly so his spit would not get into my mouth. Instead, it rolled back into my eye sockets, burning my eyes. After that experience I hated Captain K more than anyone in the world and yet I still yearned for his acceptance of me. In some ways I figured out how to retaliate, since I was not strong enough to kick his butt.

There was no way I could defend myself physically against Captain K, but as a youth I learned indirect ways to get back at him. One day on a Sunday afternoon I went to the bathroom and noticed the newspaper sitting on the floor. On the front page was the photo of a woman in a sweater. I took a black marker and drew a mustache on her face and then outlined her breast in the black ink. It was not a sexual thing for me to be drawing on her breast, I just felt like coloring with the marker that day. Once I was done, I didn't think twice about it. I just threw the paper back on the floor where I found it.

Our family had just gotten home from church. Mom was busy making lunch, which was something everyone enjoyed, especially her roast beef marinated in Claude's Sauce. Mom also made great-tasting au gratin potatoes and a green bean casserole using mushroom soup. As Mom stayed busy in the kitchen preparing lunch, my sister came storming out of the bathroom with the Sunday newspaper, holding up the photo of the lady I had colored.

Apparently my sister found my artistic enhancements offensive and so did Mom. Without warning, Mom flew across the room toward me and Captain K, who happened to be sitting near me. I knew I was in for it now, but as Mom lifted the newspaper to, I thought, smack me on the head, she then turned and started hitting Captain K on his head with it. She was screaming and yelling and asking why he would do such an awful thing.

I scrambled out of the way as Mom pounced on Captain K. She had the wrong boy. Her swats with the paper belonged to me, not him, but I did nothing to stop her from pounding him. I wanted to speak up, but it felt so good seeing my mother whopping my brother. Captain K, guarding his face, kept telling my mother that it was me that had drawn on the lady's face and breasts, but I refused to take any responsibility for it. In my mind Captain K deserved every blow he was getting and more. I suppose after all these years I should take responsibility for not being honest and trying to defend my brother from my mother's whipping with the newspaper.

My friends have told me that I must forgive Captain K in order to find my own freedom. From Captain K's perspective, he probably thought he was doing me a favor by beating the shit out of me all the time. He probably would have said that he was just trying to toughen me up. In fact what he did was destroy my sense of self-worth and for years left me incapable of defending myself from other predators. I've never found much use for forgiveness. For me, more powerful than forgiveness has been the realization that hating him was costing me too much energy and making me depressed. Once I realized what the cost was in my life, I finally let it go and have celebrated my freedom from him.

In an attempt to better understand my brother's hatred toward me, I often wondered if it was simply childhood jealousy, or had he perhaps witnessed some sort of physical and emotional abuse that taught him to abuse? In my mind, violence is something that is taught, but my mother isn't a violent person, and although my father physically abused her in the early years of their marriage, she certainly did not abuse her children. Do some people just react differently than others? I guess I will never know if Captain K witnessed things that I had not, things that taught him how to be violent by mimicking the behavior of my father, or if he inherited a gene that made him mean.

Dad and His Favorite Son

My father was built like an NFL player. He grew up in Monahans, Texas, and moved to El Paso to play college football for Texas Western. Soon after graduating from college, he taught track and football at several El Paso high schools in the early 1960s. My mother was a high school senior when they met. After she graduated from high school, they married and Mom later gave birth to Captain K. Within the next three years, my mother gave birth to three more children. I was the last of them.

My father had a vasectomy after my second sister was born, so it was a surprise when my mother became pregnant with me. Back then vasectomies were not 100 percent foolproof; my father did not want to have another child and therefore he wanted very little to do with me. Dad often pushed me away and I can recall on more than one occasion him telling me that I was not his child.

I'm not sure if he really believed that, or if he just sensed that I was somehow different from his other children. My father often called Captain K his number one son. Dad's hurtful statements like "You're not my son" and his constant focus on my older brother had a dramatic impact on my sense of self-worth.

As my self-esteem decreased, Captain K's sense of self-confidence appeared to increase. Captain K looked more like my dad than I did, and he took on Dad's muscular body frame. I had a smaller body like my mother. Since Dad didn't want much to do with me, I stayed inside and played dolls with my sisters. Dad spent time engaged with Captain K, fishing, hunting, and playing sports, the things he loved to do.

In Texas, football is a big thing and many of the coaches are revered by the community—as long as they have a winning team. Sometime after my fifth birthday Dad became the head football coach of the high school I would one day attend and we moved from a rented house on Green Knock to the home on Shaver, which my parents purchased. I loved that house and can remember the first time I entered it. The house was vacant and I can recall running from room to room. It was a very happy day for me. After making my way through the house, I recall opening the door to a two-car garage and yelling, "Hello." The garage was dark and scary. My voice echoed back and I became startled, so I quickly shut the door and ran back to my mother.

Mom and the Secrets

I later discovered the garage had a cutout in the ceiling that led to the attic. This is where I discovered my first pornographic magazine. Sometime after our family had moved in, I crawled up into the attic and under a sheet of insulation was a magazine with many pictures of naked people. The magazine was old and covered with dust and must have been left behind by the previous owners.

Sitting proudly at the kitchen table, I began to explore my new magazine. The naked men had long hair and beards and it appeared that there were more women than men in the photos. I wasn't too far into the second or third page when I felt the presence of my mother peering over my shoulder.

"What you looking at?" Mom asked.

"Some naked people," I responded.

Before I could get a better glimpse of the naked hippies, the magazine flew up into the air as if it had wings.

"Where did you find this?" Mom exclaimed as she held the magazine high above my head and out of my view.

"Up in the attic," I responded.

Mom quickly regained control of her voice and in a very kind and gentle voice she said, "Honey, I don't want you playing in the attic anymore." I don't know what she did with that magazine. It would be several more years before I would discover Captain K's *Hustler* and *Playboy* collection.

When I did discover Captain K's porn collection, I soon realized that I did not have the same interest in the magazines that all my friends did. I must have been in the fifth or sixth grade, and when Captain K went out with his friends, my friends and I would lock my bedroom door and look at all the pictures of naked women. I never understood why my friends found naked photos of women so interesting until I looked into one of his *Hustler* magazines. These photos had both men and women in them.

I was scared yet excited by what was happening to me when I would see the naked photo of a man and woman together. The first time I saw this type of photo, I experienced an erection. I didn't know what was happening to me and didn't feel comfortable talking to my parents about it. My friends were calling it a boner and literally that's what I thought I had for many years— a bone that hid inside my stomach and would pop out when I saw a photo of a naked man and woman together. I was embarrassed and ashamed of this bone and tried with very little success to push it back up where it came from. What was more confusing to me was that the little bone only appeared when a man was in the photo.

Whenever my friends and I heard my mom coming down the hall, we would quickly hide the magazines and pretend we were listening to music or we'd just start acting silly. One day I came home to discover both my parents in the bedroom that I shared with Captain K. For some reason my mother had been in our bedroom cleaning and discovered one of the magazines under Captain K's bed. She went ballistic after she had my father lift the box spring only to discover more magazines.

I'm not sure what was under that bed because my mother stopped me at the door. She then told my dad, "Clean them up and get them out of my house." Mom was outraged and I remember her telling my dad to throw them in a box or bag and to bury them in the desert, where no other kids could find them. Later that day I found Captain K's bed being removed from the bedroom. Now I had the room all to myself.

\~

The first few years we lived on Shaver were difficult for my parents. Shortly after we moved in—when I was five and a half years old—my parents began having problems in their marriage. The pressure of being a full-time coach and driving a Trailways bus to make ends meet may have been too much for Dad. My mother must have done a good job of concealing their troubles because I didn't know they had problems until one night I was awakened by my mother's screaming for help.

At first I think it's only a dream. Soon I hear another scream. I am wide awake now, hiding under my covers. I am too scared to go find out what is happening to my mother. The screams continue and I dig deeper into my bed, farther under the covers. I feel defenseless, wanting to protect Mom but paralyzed with fear.

Slowly I move one leg from under the covers onto the floor. My bed is small, a twin size. Then the other foot hits the floor. I can do this, I am saying to myself. I feel the comfort of my pajamas and know that they will protect me from the outside world.

I am dressed in them from head to toe, with my feet nestled inside the tiny foot coverings sewn onto the ends of the PJ bottoms. I slowly move to my bedroom door and peer out through the cracks between the door and door frame. My mother's screams become louder. Slowly I make my way into the hall. As I walk, I can hear the bottom of my PJs rub against the floor. I feel like I'm wearing a spacesuit, and hope it will keep me safe from what awaits me down the hall.

Afraid and alone, I make it to the end of the hall where I can peek into the den. I see my father beating my mother. She cries out for help and he tackles her like a football player. His hits are swift and deliberate like a football player tackling his opponent. My mother is much smaller than my father and she has no way to defend herself. My voice is paralyzed. I cannot speak. My father sees me out of the corner of his eye and yells at me to return to my room.

"I need water," I say.

"No, you don't," he yells.

I run back to my room and wait. My mother's cries summon me back. This time I enter the hall and see one of my sisters approaching the den. We both look at my dad beating our mother. Dad is drunk and lunges toward us. I remember my mother blocking him, allowing me to escape back to my room and get under the covers to hide. Feeling like a failure for not being able to protect Mom, I cry myself to sleep. Was I next? I wonder. Will my father be coming for me? Will my covers protect me? I cry myself to sleep but am awakened by more commotion in the house.

This time there are no screams, only the voices of several men. I slowly make my way out of my room and down the hall to the den. My mother is nowhere to be found. Police officers are searching for my father throughout the house. At one point I thought I saw my father in handcuffs. I'm not sure what happened to my father that night. I just remember being tired and relieved that he is gone. I cannot find my mother but feel that she is safe. I return to my room and crawl back under the covers. Perhaps it's just a dream. When I wake in the morning, I realize it's not. My mother, lying in her bed, is unrecognizable. Her face is swollen and her eyes, nose, and lips are all black and blue.

The horrifying beating I witnessed and the sight of my mother's shattered face still linger in my mind. I can only imagine the pain she was in.

Years later I learned that my mother never pressed charges and Dad was never actually arrested. The police officers patrolled our neighborhood throughout the evening and made sure that we were safe. In the year following the near arrest, my parents divorced and I recall visiting my father with my siblings at his apartment. I hated these visits and I despised him for what he had done to my mother. Whenever I would hear that we were going to visit him, I would cry out to my mother and cling to her neck. Looking back, I'm sure these visits were court ordered and at the time Mom had very little control over the situation.

Being divorced and raising four kids on her own was not easy for Mom. During the late 1960s and early 1970s, few social support systems were in place to help families like ours, as they are now. At one point we were at risk of losing our home and my grandparents helped us out financially.

I have a distinct memory of my mother taking me and my sisters to the Lee and Beulah Moor Foster Home. I think Captain K was with us, too. We played out on the playground while my mother spoke with the administrator. I'm not sure if my siblings knew what this place was. Somehow I did. Several years after this event, I remember riding in the backseat of the family station wagon and recognizing the building as we drove by it. When I told my dad I recalled going there, he told me that was because my mom didn't love me. Again, he reminded me that he was unsure whether I was even his child. Although I felt a sense of abandonment that day, I knew my mom loved me and was doing everything in her power to hang on to her children.

One time during my parents' divorce process, I recall my father taking us kids on a fishing trip. Other children accompanied us, but I don't recall for certain who they were. I think they may have been the children of a woman my father was dating at the time. One morning while on this camping trip, my father had asked several of us if we wanted any of the scrambled eggs still remaining in the frying pan. I raised my hand and received what was left. Shortly after my father served me the eggs, the rest of the kids got up from the campfire. Fearful that I was going to be left behind, I took the eggs and buried them in the dirt below.

As the camp area cleared, my father walked across the area where the eggs were buried and kicked them onto the ground where others could see. He came marching over to me, lifted me up by my arms, and began spanking the hell out of me. I wanted nothing more than to return home to the safety of my mother's arms.

Over the following year, my parents reconciled and Dad came back to live with us. He continued to push me away, keeping his focus on his "number one son." Captain K looked and acted like Dad. He had his bone structure and, although he was not very good at athletics, he liked to play and I think Dad really appreciated his enthusiasm for sports.

I hated sports and preferred doing things inside the house with my sisters and mother. It was always safer to stay far away from Captain K. His contempt for me was apparent and he would do anything to be the center of attention in our father's life. This went on until he graduated from high school and moved out of our house.

Even after he was gone I felt inadequate. My body was changing. Going through adolescence, I started forming little tiny fat tissue under my nipples. Since I had no muscle mass on me, it was more apparent than it was on other boys. I thought maybe Captain K was right and I was a girl growing little breasts.

One time, feeling unloved and unwanted, I ran away from home. I was going to sleep in the desert near our home, but Joey thought it would be better if I slept in the back of his father's Chevy Blazer, where no one could find me. I jumped in the back of the Blazer and Joey placed a blanket over me in case I got cold during the night.

Within a few minutes of Joey going back inside his parents' home, someone was knocking on the rear window of the Blazer. It was his mother telling me to come inside. So much for keeping a secret. Joey's mom called my mom and told her where I was. The following day I went to see a psychologist about why I ran away. I told him that I was growing breasts and was turning into a girl. The psychologist looked at my nipples and reassured me that this was common for boys who were going into puberty. I was not satisfied with his answer, so Mom took me to a surgeon, who looked at the fatty little nipples and said that if he removed the fatty tissue it would only come back. I didn't give much more attention to my fatty nipples after meeting with the surgeon because for the first time in my life I was beginning to feel free of my brother's daily harassment and I even experienced a different side of my brother that was beginning to change the way I saw myself.

I think running away must have influenced my brother's feelings toward me. One night he came back to the house to visit my parents. Mom and I were sitting at the kitchen table and Captain K sat down next to me. He asked me why I ran away and I told him because no one loved me. His eyes welled up with tears and he said, "I love you." He then told me that if I felt like running away again or needed something, all I needed to do was give him a call. With tears still in his eyes, he abruptly got up from his chair, walked outside, and drove away. Although I was touched by what he said, I didn't really know what to make of it. Years of what he probably thought was horseplay, which I experienced as abusive, had taken their toll on me. So many years of abuse do not get erased overnight, but over time things did change a little for me psychologically. I was finally feeling a sense of mastery over my own life. To some degree my sense of self-worth was improving, but the roles in our family were beginning to change, and over the years I would become resentful once again toward Captain K for not being around to care for his beloved father.

When I was in the seventh grade, Dad started showing signs of illness, which increased Mom's responsibility in raising me and my two sisters. I was having major self-esteem issues about being the oldest kid in my class. At the end of my seventh-grade year, Mom took me and my sister to a school psychologist because both of us had repeated a grade and were having difficulty being with our younger classmates. The psychologist agreed that being at grade levels not suited for our ages was affecting us emotionally. The following year I skipped the eighth grade altogether and moved into the ninth grade with the original class that I had started out with back in the first grade. My sister also advanced from the junior high that summer to the high school. It was the best move Mom could have made for us emotionally, though we were ill prepared academically for the change. Still I am grateful that the transition took place. I was now in the same age group as most of my friends and was feeling quite good about myself and my future. No one could call me a flunker anymore. In fact, most kids thought I was very smart since I had skipped the eighth grade.

Manhood

Working at Griggs Restaurant provided me many opportunities to grow and mature as a young man. I met a waitress there named Carmen, a high school graduate and a woman eager to introduce a timid sixteen-year-old into manhood. I was eager to lose my virginity too, wanting to do it before my friends did.

Both of my sisters were sitting in the den one night when I walked in and announced that I would be sneaking out of the house. (Never tell your sister a secret if you want it to be kept a secret.) Feeling great and ready to rock, I put on a tired face and quietly walked into my parents' bedroom. Mom and Dad were already in bed when I told my mom to make sure that I was up early in the morning so I could make it to the restaurant early enough to make tortillas.

After I shut their bedroom door, I began to walk to my bedroom. Both of my sisters followed me. The oldest one threatened to tell Mom and Dad that I was going to sneak out and the other simply acted indifferent. Eventually the girls left me alone. I stepped onto my waterbed and untwisted the lightbulb in the center of the ceiling. I then filled my bed with pillows and blankets to give the shape of my body. My thought was that if Mom did check on me, she would look into the bedroom, think she was seeing me sleeping, and then go back to bed. Once I had my bed set up, I crawled out the window and shut it behind me.

Carmen was waiting for me at the end of the street in her father's black Ford LTD. I climbed into the front seat and in horror watched my mother, father, and sisters walk out onto our front porch. Mom had installed floodlights around the house and with a click of the switch our house was illuminated in white light.

I couldn't believe my sisters had ratted on me. I looked at Carmen with excitement and fear. She asked if I wanted to go back home, but I realized that no matter what I did I was going to be grounded for life. So I lay down in the front seat of Carmen's car, resting my head on her lap. She drove slowly by the front of our house and I could hear the entire family calling out my name. After I got over the humiliation of it all, Carmen drove us to the 7-Eleven on the east side of town. She bought a bottle of MD 20/20 and then drove us out to the desert.

Eventually I found myself in the middle of nowhere listening to Carmen tell me ghost stories. I was a little scared, but more nervous about making love for the first time. I wasn't sure what to do and none of it seemed very natural. Then Carmen pulled off her shirt. Wow! I knew what I was seeing, but I certainly didn't know what I was going to do with them. Nervous, excited, and feeling a bit nauseated from the MD 20/20, I soon found myself in the backseat with Carmen, totally naked. I'm not sure if it lasted a minute or two minutes, but the entire experience happened faster than I could recite the alphabet, yet it was exhilarating and well worth sneaking out for.

When I arrived home, all the lights in the interior and exterior of our house were off. I walked to the side of the house to crawl through my bedroom window only to discover Mom had locked it. I then went to my sister's window and knocked. She slowly opened her window and said she wanted nothing to do with me and my escape. Before I knew it, Patches, our dog, began to bark. My sister shut her window, leaving me outdoors.

I sat on the front porch, still feeling a little drunk from the

MD 20/20, and began wondering how on God's earth I was going to get into my house. Then it dawned on me that I had a key to the front door. I couldn't believe I hadn't thought of that earlier. I reached into my pocket, pulled out the key, and quietly opened the door. Patches began to bark again and the entire house echoed with her roar. Interestingly enough, no lights turned on. I assumed that my dad spoke to my mom about me gaining my independence and they decided not to respond to my getaway.

I walked into my bedroom and crawled into my king-size water bed. My mind was clouded from the alcohol that I had consumed and the room felt as if it was spinning. Then all of a sudden the water-filled mattress began to sway back and forth as if someone were in the bed with me. Apparently Mom got tired of waiting up for me to return home, so she had fallen asleep in my bed. Mom then crawled out the other side of the bed.

Before I knew it, the hall light went on, out came the Bible, and Mom stood in my doorway reading aloud one scripture passage after another. I wasn't listening. I just wanted the room to stop spinning. I don't know if she suspected where I had been or what I had been doing and I don't think she cared. She was just angry that I lied to her and snuck out. That was totally out of character for me. It would be expected from my sister but not from me.

I didn't really care what Mom was spewing at me that night. My room was still spinning and I was busy thinking about how I was going to brag to all my friends about having sex with an older woman.

The following morning I woke up and got ready for work. My parents were in the kitchen and I was doing my best to keep my distance from Mom. She was the disciplinarian in our family and I didn't want all hell to break loose first thing in the morning. Running late for work, I moved quickly through the kitchen, skipping breakfast altogether. Mom barely acknowledged me as I walked out the front door.

Once I arrived at work, I was still feeling a little lightheaded from the MD 20/20 in my bloodstream. I had cottonmouth, and my body, especially my lower legs, really ached. I think I might have pulled some muscles when climbing out of my bedroom window or out of the backseat of Carmen's car.

The restaurant was busy that morning and Mr. Duke was in one of his micromanaging moods, so there were very few moments in which I could tell the other busboys about my Don Juan experience the night before. Busboys always showed up before the waitresses because we had to make the tortillas, but the tortilla machine was loud, so we couldn't really talk when we were making them. Mr. Duke kept coming in and out of the room as if he knew the other busboys and I were up to something.

After the machine was turned off, the other boys gathered around to hear my story. Everyone knew that the night before, Carmen was going to pick me up and that I was sneaking out of my house to discover what it meant to be a real man. Just as I was about to give them the full details, Mr. Duke walked in yapping and yapping about the front of the restaurant not being clean. Suddenly my audience was disbursed, and I was cleaning the front of the restaurant.

By the time we had mopped and swept the front entry, the other waitresses had arrived and so did my lady friend. She grinned as she passed me in the front entry. I could tell Mr. Duke knew something was up but none of us were talking. Every time I started to tell the guys about my sexual experience, Mr. Duke would show up. Finally I gave up on telling anyone about what had happened and just got busy working.

Suddenly I heard a few of the waitress giggling at the waitress station. Carmen had spilled the beans. Within minutes, news of the loss of my virginity had been spread all over the restaurant.

In some ways I felt like a hero when I passed some of the other guys and they gave me high fives. In other ways I felt dirty, as If I had done something wrong. A few of the elderly women cooking in the kitchen looked at me with disappointment.

I don't think Mr. Duke ever discovered what all the talk was about that day. He asked me if I wanted to work a double shift and I said yes because I didn't want to go home and face my mother. Surprisingly, when I did get home that night Mom didn't say a word to me about the night before. Instead she was sitting in the chair, like usual, next to the fireplace with a cup of hot tea in one hand and her Bible in the other. *Maybe all hell is not going to break loose,* I thought. Dad was acting like his usual passive and disengaged self. Mom was still a bit distant but not angry. She looked hurt. She never asked me where I had been all night. Knowing that I was with an older woman would have only upset her and gotten Carmen in trouble. Giving a minor alcohol and engaging in a sexual act with him would have landed Carmen in jail if my mother had found out. As protective of me as Mom was, she would have thrown charges at the waitress. I didn't want to get Carmen in trouble and I certainly didn't want to cause my mom any more stress.

Dad's Health

Mom was under enough stress. Dad was still working, but his health was beginning to deteriorate. I remember being only seventeen when I walked into the kitchen and heard Mom say in a quavering voice, "Your dad can't see." She was standing in front of the stove, stirring a pot of Malt-O-Meal.

"What do you mean, he can't see?" I exclaimed.

Mom said nothing. She took a deep breath and held back her tears as she poured the hot cereal into separate bowls for me and my sister. "Hurry up and eat. You're running late for school."

I sat down next to Dad, who was already sitting at the kitchen table with his shoulders and head drooping. Dad had had diabetes for quite a while and had undergone a number of eye surgeries. Now, for the first time, I realized that his diabetes was not going to get any better. He was beginning to surrender to its symptoms. This moment was a turning point, not only for him, but also for my entire family. There would be no more eye surgeries, and a very long journey had begun. After Dad was declared legally blind, his ill health forced him into early retirement. A year later he was placed on kidney dialysis.

This isn't supposed to happen to a man in his forties, I thought to myself. *Dad is a strong man—a high school football coach and teacher.*

Over the years, my second oldest sister and I assisted Mom as Dad's primary caregivers. We did everything from cooking and cleaning to bathing, dressing, grooming, and toileting him. My sister helped Mom with the daily insulin injections and the changing of Dad's dialysis bags. I would often cut his toenails and give him foot massages, and my sister and I helped Mom by running errands and by taking Dad to his countless doctor appointments. Mom did not like leaving Dad alone, so we stayed home most of the time. Although I considered my father emotionally absent during my childhood, he had provided for our family financially. We even went on family vacations when I was a child and for the most part they were pleasant. Once Dad became ill, there were no more family vacations or other enjoyable activities that most families were able to do.

We all pitched in because we loved Dad and also felt a sense of obligation to care for him. But over time I felt the sacrifice was too much and began to feel burnt out. I was angry at Dad for getting sick and angry at God for making him sick. I was angry with my mom for staying with a man who had abused her in the early years of their marriage. I was upset with my older siblings for not being in town to help with our father's care. Most of all I was angry at myself for feeling resentful.

In many ways Dad was a good man. There were very few times I can ever recall my father speaking ill of others. After Captain K left the house, Dad and I became much closer than we had ever been. It was obvious by my appearance that I was his child, so he had stopped teasing me about belonging to someone else.

I did love my dad but at the same time I resented both him and my older brother. Here I was, helping my mom care for my dad, a man who had wanted nothing to do with me for most of my life. Yet my older brother, his "number one son," only stopped by once in a while and didn't engage in any of the daily caregiving duties. My resentment had less to do with the caregiving responsibilities than with the missed opportunities to do things that my friends all took for granted with their dads.

Even though as a child I preferred hanging out with my mother more than I did with my dad, I felt cheated. My confused teenage mind thought the sexual abuse I experienced as a young child and Dad's absence had something to do with my feeling confused about my sexual orientation. There was a part of me that thought that if I went fishing and hunting and had a strong male role in my life, I would develop a heterosexual orientation. Now that Dad had time to spend with me, his illness was preventing him from teaching a young man what he needed to learn in order to mature into adulthood.

If I needed help working on my car, I had to go to a friend's house and ask his dad for help. Sometimes I would look at my dad and think that the only reason he was around me at all was because he was sick and didn't have a choice. Then, over time, my perception began to change about caring for Dad. As our roles were changing, he was becoming more like my child than my father. I didn't want to hang out with my friend's dad anymore. I wanted to hang out with my dad and bond with him.

Having my own dad was better than sharing someone else's dad. Mr. Duke told me that his kids were jealous of the time he spent with me and that he needed to be more mindful of their needs. I was surprised when he told me this but I also honored what he was saying and really appreciated the fact that his kids were his first priority. Although my dad lay in bed all day, I no longer felt judged by him and began feeling a greater sense of security.

Illness was also changing Dad. He was becoming more engaged in my life. When I got home from school, he asked questions about my classes. Sometimes he said nothing but let me rant about what was going on with some of my friends.

When I was a junior in high school, I became the president of a chapter of DECA, Distributive Education Clubs of America. Having this title made me feel really good about myself, so I asked my friend Brent if he would like to join. Initially he thought it was a great idea and I went over to his house to tell his parents about the program. Although they listened to me share my story about the program with interest, the following day Brent told me that his parents didn't want him to use his elective credits for the class.

Brent was really smart, much smarter than I, and I got the sense that DECA wasn't for the really bright kids but for the kids who weren't making it in the advanced classes. Brent didn't tell me that, but I pretty much figured it out when his parents didn't let him sign up.

Dad liked DECA and affirmed my participation in it and that made me feel good. Brent and I stopped working at the restaurant and Mr. Stevens, a man from our church, got us jobs at Kmart. Mr. Stevens was the general manager and got jobs for many of the youth from the congregation. I don't remember what area Brent worked in, but I worked in layaway and hated it.

A Time Away

After high school graduation I didn't know what I was going to do with myself. I grew up thinking I wasn't college material and had decided that college wasn't going to be an option for me. Captain K and my oldest sister were both living in the Dallas area, so I joined them. I lived with Captain K for a short stint and worked a few dead-end jobs. Looking back, it seems a little weird that I would opt to live with my brother given our history, but deep down I admired his confidence and by this time he wasn't beating me up all the time. By September I had returned to El Paso. I moved back in with my parents and continued to help Mom take care of Dad's needs.

Returning to El Paso was somewhat humiliating for me. Most of the kids I grew up with came from money and they were all attending college outside of El Paso. Not only was I not attending college, but I was living in my parents' home and had returned to Kmart as a cashier. This time I only lasted there a few months.

Coming Out

Coming back home also brought up some of the painful childhood memories. Confusion about my sexuality was intensifying and I felt as though I was going to have a nervous breakdown. I didn't know any gay people, yet I knew I was attracted to other men my age. This was confusing to me because I didn't want to be gay and I certainly didn't want to go to hell as my religion said I would. I didn't know who to talk to about it. I couldn't tell my parents. Mom was extremely homophobic. I wrestled with ideas about killing myself, but I couldn't do that either because I believed that people who kill themselves go to hell. My Christian religion was tearing me apart psychologically and I felt completely trapped.

Finally I went over to Joey's house and told his mom that I was having these feelings that my friends were not having. I told her I thought I might be gay but that I didn't know for sure. At the same time, I was thinking that I was the only person in the world who was gay and someday someone would make a movie about it. She listened to me calmly and told me that she didn't know much about being gay or what caused a person to be gay. She did know my history with my father and I think she believed that if I met the right woman I would grow into having a heterosexual identity.

It wasn't long after that discussion that I heard of a made-for-TV movie called *Consenting Adults*. It was the story of a young man struggling with his sexual orientation. I asked Joey's mom if I could watch it at her house and she said yes. That night I discovered that I was not the only gay person in the world and that there would be no movie made about me. I was also relieved to learn there were others out there just like me. After the show I walked back over to my parents' home, but I was not going to tell them about what I had just seen on TV. Mom had too much on her plate and Dad was becoming sicker. This was the last thing they needed to deal with.

When I went home that night and opened the front door, my second oldest sister greeted me and motioned me to her bedroom. She said, "Mom and Dad watched a show on TV to-night about this gay kid and they think you might be gay too. They're going to ask you about it." Before my sister could ask me any other questions, I told her I thought I was gay. She looked surprised and then said, "Well, I still love you, but the Bible says you're going to hell."

By this time I could hear my mother calling out my name. "Grant, come in here. Your father and I want to speak with you." I didn't want to go in there, so I told them I needed to go to bed. I looked in the den and saw my mother with her cup of tea and her Bible that she read almost every night before going to bed. I think she had been looking up scripture passages about homo-sexuals. My sister disappeared back into her bedroom and my dad stayed resting in his pajamas on the sofa.

"Your father and I watched a movie tonight and there were some similarities between you and the young man in the movie," Mom said.

Before I could think about it I blurted out, "I *am* like him."

I think my response caught Mom off guard.

"What do you mean you are like him?"

I couldn't say the word "gay"; I just said I was like that guy. At first my mother looked like she was in a state of disbelief and was going to faint. She fell to the floor and started crying and then screaming. It was as if she had just heard that one of her children had been murdered or killed tragically in a car ac-cident. Mom quickly grabbed her Bible and began to read all the passages that have been written about and quoted against homosexuals. Each time she read one it was like she was using scripture as a weapon against me and I was being stabbed in the heart by her words. I felt that my mother would rather have heard that I was killed in a tragic car accident than to learn that I might be gay.

I knew what I was telling her was going to hurt her, but I

never dreamed she would respond the way she did. She was having a breakdown right in front of me and Dad.

"Don't tell anyone until we really know what is going on with you."

Mom went into the kitchen and I heard some dishes breaking. Mom was out of control and my dad finally sat up and snapped at her. He yelled out something about me still being their son. After my mother's rant she came over to me, still crying. She reached over and hugged me and then said everything was going to be OK and that she would get me the help I needed to be straight. Although she had good intentions, her actions would prove to be psychologically harmful.

There was something about telling my parents that finally set me free. Of course that was short-lived. The following day my mom went to see our family physician and I went along. Doctor Tubbs was the doctor who had delivered me almost nineteen years earlier. I didn't really know any other doctors but him. Mom went into his office before I did. I'm not sure what he told her, but I assume he told her that nothing was wrong with me and to calm down. He sent my mom out to the waiting room and the nurse then called me in. Dr. Tubbs gave me a brief physical and asked me if I was doing OK. My time with him only lasted a few minutes and I was back out in the waiting room with my mom.

I know my mother loved me, yet she was horrified at the idea of my being gay. She didn't like me talking with others about being gay. It was embarrassing to her. She thought I was just going through a stage. Everyone had a theory as to why I was gay: his father didn't love him; he had a dominant mother figure; his older brother beat him up; or he was sexually abused as a little boy. I was halfway convinced myself that if only my relationship with my father came full circle, then I would evolve into a heterosexual.

I felt guilty and shameful for being me and I wanted so badly for the gayness in me to leave. Dr. Tubbs had given me the name of a Catholic woman who claimed that her son was once gay and became heterosexual. At the time I thought there were some gay people who were born gay and some who were formed gay by the way they were raised or because of their life experiences. I agreed to meet with her at her house. For over an hour we read scripture and prayed. She told me Satan had entered my body and was making me gay. She also said she knew some ladies who could help cast the demon out.

I agreed to connect with this group of women from an evangelical church who were serving at Fort Bliss. They said they were "ex-lesbians" and they too affirmed that I had a gay demon and that it needed to be cast out. Knowing how Mom felt about my sexuality, I went over to their house one day. Several other people from their church were also present. The ladies had me sit down in their family room and invited the Holy Spirit in to cast out the demon.

Church members began pouring oil on me and praying in tongues, demanding that the gay demon leave at once. What they were doing was kind of freaking me out but I wanted so badly to be straight that I was willing to do anything. When I left there, however, I was still gay.

While Working at the Marriott

In January of 1985, a short while after coming out, I got a job at the El Paso Marriott Hotel. Shawn, Mr. Duke's daughter, introduced me to a girlfriend of hers whose mother, Mrs. Eaton, was the front desk manager. I applied for the clerk's job and was hired. I liked it and I thought that now my life was going somewhere. I enrolled in a local two-year college with a focus on hotel and motel administration. At times it appeared as if things were going to get better for my family too. Then, out of nowhere, another crisis came crashing in on us.

One night, while caring for my father, my mother began to experience severe abdominal cramps. I rushed her to the hospital and later that evening surgeons worked to repair a ruptured intestine. Her condition was life threatening and it was unclear if she was going to survive her illness. It was also apparent that she would not be able to care for my father until her full recovery.

Because I was working full-time at the Marriott, Dad's care needs were too great for me to handle, so he also was admitted to the hospital. I spent several weeks going between hospital floors, caring for both Mom and Dad, while waiting anxiously for Mom to recover fully. Mom's recovery continued after her release from the hospital and we were very thankful to have the support of a home health aide to help us care for Dad.

I was amazed to watch as my mother recovered quickly from her own illness in order to offer my dad the care he needed. She credits her survival and recovery to friends, family, and the nuns at the hospital praying for her, along with the excellent team of Jewish doctors who were caring for this conservative Baptist woman.

Indeed, when we are sick, we need the skill of doctors and the prayers of many to recover, but we must also discover our own resiliency to achieve wellness. For my mom, this resiliency came from her ability to know and nurture herself. It was her example that taught me the importance of self-love when caring for others. But I still had a difficult time applying that self-love to myself. I didn't like who I was and I was still struggling with questions about my sexuality.

I met a few people who worked at the college and the hotel who were gay, which caused me to think more about my own sexuality. Of course I was not going to come out publicly because I was a Christian and had been led to believe that Christians are not gay. I was told by my church and by other Christians I knew that if only I prayed more about it and truly asked God to take away the gay demon, then I would be straight. I begged and pleaded for God to make me straight but nothing changed for me. Like many gay people counseled by well-meaning Christians who condemned gayness, I was suffering deep confusion and anxiety. It disturbs me to this day that many people like me, influenced by this kind of pressure, develop severe psychological problems, which in some cases lead to suicide.

Working at the hotel and attending the two-year college introduced me to all sorts of different lifestyles, and my perception of the world was beginning to change. I was yearning to have more independence from my family. A guy older than I who was affiliated with the college took an interest in me and encouraged me to model for the school's program in merchandising and design. The school hired me to model at a few shows held at Cielo Vista Mall and Bassett Center.

Mom didn't mind the fact that I was modeling, but she made it very clear on several occasions that she didn't like some of the people I was hanging out with. I dismissed her concern as being overprotective.

I wish I had listened a little harder to her the night the older guy from the school and his partner invited me over for dinner. These two guys made me uncomfortable though I didn't really know why. Years later I would remember the horrors of what happened that night, which I had quickly blocked out of my memory. But for now it was just a night for me to forget.

Not long after having dinner at their house I decided to quit school. My front office manager, Mrs. Eaton, had transferred earlier to Baltimore, Maryland, and called to see if I would be interested in working at the hotel there. Although Dad was still very sick, Mom had fully recovered and I was ready to leave El Paso to claim my independence. I flew to Baltimore and began my new position at the Baltimore Marriott Inner Harbor Hotel. For the first few weeks, I lived with Mrs. Eaton and her daughters in a small row house. Eventually I saved enough money to rent an apartment on top of the New York Sewing Machine store.

Still trying to cast out the gay demon in me, I joined an Exodus International Group, made up of well-meaning Christians trying to heal others of their gayness. I only attended a few meetings and then realized that taking part in this group was getting me nowhere. Most of the men and women in the program were still gay and seemed to be in immense pain over trying to accept themselves. Although I was coming to terms with my own sexual orientation, I was also very homophobic. One night a somewhat flamboyant guest checked into the hotel. I made a comment to one of the servers about how gay the man was, and it got back to him. He was furious. The following day I was working the night shift and he suddenly appeared at the front desk. He asked me to meet him down at the end of the counter. I had no idea I was in trouble, but he was very pissed. He told me in no uncertain terms that his sexuality was none of my business. I'm sure he said much more than that, but I did not hear him. All I know is that he ended with, "I'm a Marriott Marquis member and could have your job if I wanted it." I stood there in a state of shock.

The following morning I told my supervisor what had happened. She didn't seem too concerned and I never saw the man again. I had learned something important from him, though— that it was possible for a gay man to stand up for himself.

When Mrs. Eaton transferred to another hotel, I found myself homesick and missing my family. A few months later I was back at home in El Paso, caring for my father and working at Griggs again.

Dad's Death

On a Sunday night I came home to discover my mother standing next to my father. The only thing I can recall her saying that night is, "You need to say good-bye to your dad."

As Mom left the room, I fell to my knees and held my father's lifeless body in my arms. I felt the presence of angels in the room taking Dad's spirit home. In that moment my resentment disappeared and I would have done anything to have him back.

Neighbors filled our house as our family mourned Dad's death. Once the neighbors left, Mom and I stayed with Dad's body until the staff from the funeral home arrived.

I saw something that night I wish I had never seen. The men from the funeral home entered my parents' home dressed in fine dark suits. The expression on their faces was stoic as they lifted my father's body into the dark bag, the kind you see in movies at crime scenes. As Dad was dying, he had curled up into a fetal position. The men had to stretch out his body in order to get him in the dark bag. I thought I heard his bones cracking as they lifted him into the bag. Once he was in the bag, they zipped it up and began moving toward me. I backed out of the room and into the hall. Once the men had him on the stretcher, they had to make a tight turn in the hall and accidentally dropped his body on the floor. My mother gasped. The men then pushed his body out of the house and I followed them, screaming with the irrationality of shock and grief, "Open the bag! He doesn't like the dark."

Caring for my father at a young age transformed who I would become as an adult and taught me the value of compassion, patience, and understanding. Eventually, this experience led me to work in human services for a nonprofit organization, where I became a manager of independent housing communities for seniors and people who have chronic physical and mental disabilities. The residents I served included people with paraplegia and quadriplegia, some from birth and others as the result of illness or injury. There were also residents with schizophrenia, bipolar disorder, and other mental health issues. I thought I would be teaching these people how to become more self-reliant, but instead they taught me how to be more authentic.

I felt a bond with the people who lived in the community I managed. Since I had cared for my father and had suffered with depression myself, I could identify with how many of the residents felt. It was obvious that many of those who were old or had a disability felt like they did not belong. I sure knew what that felt like.

Coming back to Shaver Street after all these years and looking at my childhood home was making me feel empty inside. I wasn't feeling the closure I had felt earlier when I had visited Cielo Vista School. Maybe I was feeling empty because no matter what work I was doing to heal, it wasn't going to bring back my father, or maybe it was because I wasn't living in El Paso when my mother sold our family home. I still had visions of my parents' personal belongings being inside the house, even though those items had been moved several years earlier and a new family was living in the space I once called home.

That house brought back a lot of old memories, some good and some bad. In many ways I was grateful for my time growing up there. It's where my parents taught me what it means to be human by the experiences I had growing up. I learned about pain, disappointment, and resilience. I learned that life isn't always fair, yet in comparison to most Americans kids I had it pretty good. I never went without food, clothing, or shelter, and I had parents who were engaged in my upbringing. We sat down together as a family for dinner every night and I never had a Christmas without presents under the six-foot, artificial white Christmas tree my parents put up every year.

I can recall waking up on Christmas morning to handmade red velvet stockings Mom had sewn for me and my siblings. Each stocking had a tiny "Bible," no larger than an inch or two, sewn onto the front side, just underneath our stitched-in names. The stocking was full of fruit, nuts, and new underwear and socks. Christmas was a joyous time for my family in many ways, and yet the holiday of Christmas left me with many questions and often a sense of emptiness.

When I was growing up, I would never have publicly questioned my parents about my Christian faith, but now as an adult I am able to say, *It just doesn't make sense to me.* I can hear my mother's voice saying, "It doesn't have to make sense, it's all about having faith." But my ability to reason things out doesn't support the faith I was raised with.

And yet, as I now revisited some of the people and places that had shaped me during those years, I realized some things I could only understand after many years of being away and going through a deep process of healing. My parents were good parents, but parenting is a difficult task and parents make decisions based on what they know and the resources they have available at the time to care for their children. Being raised Christian and helping to care for my father taught me the importance of reaching out to others who are less fortunate. I also think whatever positive or negative experiences I had as a child now serve me in better understanding others who may not share the same faith.

Ending the Day

It was getting to be late afternoon and I still needed to meet Coach and his wife, Joan, for dinner over at Jaxon's on Airway Boulevard not far from where I grew up. Coach had worked with my dad for many years and also taught my sister and me biology in high school. At one time he and his wife were very good friends with my parents. My sister and I grew up with their kids, and after graduating from high school, stayed close with their daughters.

I said good-bye to my childhood home and drove over to the restaurant to meet them. Things hadn't changed much for Coach and Joan; they looked great and were upbeat and optimistic. They had remained athletic and, outside of their hair turning a little salt-and-pepper, they looked the same to me as when I left El Paso years earlier. They were happy to see me and I was happy to see them. They knew I was coming to town to confront something, but they weren't aware of the details.

Once Coach and his wife were seated on the other side of the table from me at Jaxon's, I showed them the impact letter that I planned to read to the Wrestler. My impact letter talked about my abuse: what happened, how the Wrestler hurt me, and how I felt about what he did to me. After they read it silently, a few more moments of silence followed. By the expression on his face, I sensed that Coach was really mad, not at me but at the Wrestler. "Why didn't you come and tell us about this before?" he asked.

"I was too embarrassed," I told them. Neither of them knew who the Wrestler was, and they expressed some concern about my safety in confronting him.

"Don't worry," I assured them. "I'll be OK. I have several other advocates in town helping me with this."

While we ate, we reflected on old times. After dinner I hugged Coach and Joan good-bye and drove to my hotel.

I was tired and still anxious about being in public where I might be easily seen by anyone in pursuit of me. I had booked a room under my grandfather's name at the Howard Johnson Hotel. It was the hotel that out-of-town guests always stayed in when visiting my parents. I was familiar with the hotel and thought I would be safe there.

When I drove up, I noticed a chain-link fence on the west side of the building facing Hawkins Street. I had flashbacks of the fence on the playground at Cielo Vista. Then I had another flashback of the chain-link fence in the parking garage at a downtown hotel, the one where the Wrestler raped me. Now I was beginning to feel uncomfortable about sleeping at the Howard Johnson. The hotel was run down and old but it was cheap, so I decided to check in. I would not leave until morning. I didn't want the Wrestler or one of his guys to be waiting for me outside or to gain access to the room while I was out visiting friends.

CHAPTER THREE

Day 2

Preparing to Confront, Thursday, April 6, 2006

My mind and body were not in harmony when I woke up Thursday morning. I had not slept well and my body was pleading for more sleep, yet my mind was planning out the day's events. I wouldn't be meeting with the Wrestler until the following day, Friday, at 2:00 p.m., yet I continued to be worried that he or someone else might be following me.

The room I was staying in at the Howard Johnson was located in the northwest corner of the hotel, the corner farthest away from the office and night staff. I asked the desk clerk for a room closer to the office. He looked uninterested in reassigning my room number and the last thing I wanted to do was call attention to myself by looking scared, so I took the room I'd been assigned.

In an attempt to hide from the Wrestler, I tried concealing my identity by checking in under my grandfather's name and upon checking out, I planned to have the front desk clerk change the reservation back to my legal name. I thought that if there were any foul play at least the police would be able to track where I had been prior to confronting the Wrestler. I checked out of my room at 10:06 a.m. and paid $63.77 for my night of insomnia. I thought that price was a bargain, but if you saw the room I was staying in, you would probably disagree. The hotel was old and needed to be renovated or knocked down.

Visiting the Cemetery

After leaving the hotel, I drove to the north side of town to visit the cemetery where my father and maternal grandmother were buried. They are buried next to each other in the mausoleum located right behind the chapel. The chapel was not how I remembered it the day my father was buried, November 28, 1987. That day it was full of activity. Outside the front of the chapel were the hearse and several black limousines. The front chapel doors were open, overflowing with people trying to get a glimpse of what was happening inside. The chapel was filled with family, friends, professional acquaintances, and students Dad had taught throughout the years.

Now silence filled the chapel and mausoleum as I stood staring up at my father's and grandmother's tombs. I wanted to reach out and touch the surface of Dad's tomb, but it was at least ten to twelve feet from the ground, above my reach.

Dad would be proud of me for coming back to confront the Wrestler, I thought to myself. Closing my eyes, I began to meditate and give thanks for the new personal strength I had discovered, when suddenly I was startled by a whooshing sound shooting past my ear. Goose bumps covered my body and I was spooked. Fear took over as I turned around and looked for the Wrestler or anyone else who might have followed me into the mausoleum. This would be a great place for someone to kill me, because no one was near, nor would anyone be able to hear through the cement and stone walls.

My heart began to race, but then suddenly slowed down when I realized the scare had come from nothing more than a bird flying past me and into the enormous corridors of the mausoleum. Looking down at the floor, I noticed bird shit on the carpet and marble stone in front of my father's tomb. I had to laugh because my father once described people who hurt others or take them for granted as being like birds. "They just walk around shitting on people and then fly away. They don't think twice about it." I wondered if the Wrestler ever thought about what he had done to me so many years ago and what he must be feeling about my coming back to confront him. I also wondered if my father had become some sort of angelic being and whether the bird shit was just a subtle reminder that he was there to protect me in spirit.

For a moment, I thought I must have let the bird in when I opened the doors to the mausoleum, but then I noticed several pieces of stained glass missing from one of the windows. The bird must have gained entry through one of the holes. I walked over to the window and could hear more birds chirping on the other side of it. The frame holding the window in place was rusting out at the bottom. The cemetery and mausoleum had been almost impeccable when my mother's friend, Mrs. Anderson, managed it. Apparently after she retired, things fell into disrepair.

I walked around the mausoleum in search of a small ladder or chair that I could use to replace the silk flowers at the front of my family's tombs. The night before, Joan had agreed to meet me later that afternoon at Hobby Lobby and arrange new flowers for each of the vases at the tombs. Looking feverishly around the corridors of the mausoleum, I still had the fear that someone or something was going to jump out and get me. However, the current condition of the mausoleum was more irritating than the fear of being killed inside it. When I first went inside, the front metal doors had squeaked when I opened them and clashed harshly against each other when they shut. I had worried that they might not open when I was ready to leave and I could be locked in overnight. As I now continued to search for something to stand on, I walked outside to survey the exterior of the building and noticed the stucco was cracking in some places and the paint on the exterior trim of the building was chipping off.

When I went back inside the mausoleum, I noticed the strong astringent smell of the insecticide used inside the building. I didn't see any bugs, but I assumed there must be a bug problem, or the smell wouldn't be so strong. Maybe the bugs only come out at night, I thought, and spend their days eating away at our loved ones. That thought grossed me out and I found myself growing resentful toward my mother for putting Dad here. In retrospect, I suppose the anger at my mother was not really about how she buried my father. After all, bugs eat bodies even when they are buried in the ground.

Resentment was not going to get these flowers replaced, so I continued my search for something to stand on to remove the vases. Unable to find anything, I discovered a long stick with a two-prong slot on one end that looked like it was made to install and remove the small flower vases on each tomb. Grabbing the long stick and lifting it up, I positioned the stick up against the flower vases one at a time and grabbed them off of my father's and grandmother's tombs. I took them with me so that Joan could create a new floral design from the flowers that we were going to select at Hobby Lobby. Vases in hand, I made a quick dash to my rental car that was parked out front and drove away.

Although relieved to get away from the cemetery, I felt guilty about leaving my father's body to spend eternity in the rundown mausoleum. *If it looks like this now, what is it going to look like a hundred years from now? What if El Paso gets hit with a tornado and the winds blow down the mausoleum, leaving his casket wide open for thieves?* My thoughts returned to wishing we had buried him six feet down in an oak box and then just covered him with dirt. At the time of his death, it seemed like a good idea to have him buried next to my grandmother. The burial plot was free. My mother's parents had bought the tombs for themselves years earlier but after my grandmother died, my grandfather remarried and was no longer interested in being buried next to my grandmother.

My Grandparents

Although I have very few memories of my grandmother, I do remember that she had pale-white skin and fire-red hair. She wore pointed metal glasses with stones embedded on the outer frame that looked like diamonds and she liked to drink and smoke. My grandmother was an educated professional who taught school. She was also an alcoholic and often embarrassed my mother with her drunken walk and slurred speech.

I was seven years old when my grandmother died on January 5, 1973. My grandfather called our house and I answered the phone. With an enthusiastic voice he said, "Hello, Tiger," then asked for my mom. I called out to Mom and she came to the phone. Suddenly a look of confusion came over her face as she tried to comprehend what my grandfather was trying to tell her. Unable to understand him, she ended the phone call. She then called him back in an attempt to better understand what he was saying. I'm not sure if she cried or not, but I remember our routine changed that morning.

Mom left our house in a rush and drove over to meet with her dad to view the lifeless body of the redhead she had called Mom, a woman she resented greatly. My grandfather had found my grandmother in bed, dead. With no warning, she died in her sleep. Mom thinks she died of cirrhosis of the liver, brought on by the abuse of alcohol.

I still have the twin-size bed she died in. I've been holding on to it for years, hoping my niece would want it, but she has expressed no interest. Mom says it's a replica of one that was in *Gone with the Wind*, which is the only reason I've kept it all these years.

My grandparents owned a house full of antiques, located on the edge of the Franklin Mountains on Galloway Drive, in the historic El Paso neighborhood known as Kern Place. The house was typical of houses in the area, but what made it special to my siblings and me was a little cement pond in the backyard, where we often spent summer days. Facing the pond was a glassed-in patio where my grandmother would sit in her recliner and watch us play. In one hand she often held a drink; in the other, a cigarette.

One day when I was in preschool, I was watching TV on a sofa on the patio. My grandmother was sitting in a recliner to my left. I heard my grandfather's grumbling voice as he walked into the room. When I looked up, he was handing her a drink. He then started to rub her shoulders and neck area. I could see that my grandmother was not wearing a bra or blouse. This was the first time I had ever seen a woman's breasts and I had no idea what I was looking at. Later that night I mentioned it to my mother and after that day I don't recall my grandparents ever babysitting my siblings or me again.

Throughout the years and during my own recovery, Mom shared with me the facts and stories that had most affected her life. Hearing these stories helped me to understand why my mother became the person she is today.

The relationship my mother had with her parents was tumultuous, to say the least. From the time of her birth, my mother was raised in a nursery called Wheeler's Children's Cottage, Boarding Home and Day Nursery, located at 4220 Oxford Street. The building is long gone because of urbanization and the construction of a new freeway. Both of Mom's parents were educated professionals and had the financial resources to care for a child, so it was never clear to me why Mom spent her childhood years growing up in a nursery.

Mother's inspiration at the boarding home was Miss Mable E. Wheeler, who was a registered nurse. Miss Wheeler had moved to El Paso from New York for health reasons. She adopted three children from different families and opened the nursery. These children were grown by the time Mom went to the nursery in June of 1941. But many more came. None lived there full-time like Mom. Mom called Miss Wheeler "Mother Wheeler." She lived with her full-time until age nine and a half. From 1951 to 1953, Mom lived part-time at the nursery and part-time with her parents, two alcoholics who were physically and emotionally violent. Mom was in the fifth grade when Mother Wheeler fell ill and had to close the nursery. Mom then had to come to terms with having to live full-time with her parents.

One day, when Mom was a child, she was out playing with a cousin, who told her that she was adopted. Mother didn't know what that word meant, so she ran inside the house to ask her grandmother about it. The adults in the house told her it didn't mean anything, so for the most part, Mom dismissed the comment. And yet the memory of that event would haunt her for years to come.

Apparently, all of Mom's relatives knew about the adoption, but since it was never talked about around my mother, she grew up thinking she was the biological child of the man and woman she called Mom and Dad. Over the years Mom's relationship with her parents remained strained. Eventually, at the age of twenty-nine, she lost trust in everyone when her parents confirmed that she indeed was adopted. After hearing this news, my mother, struggling to raise four children under the age of ten, was distraught. She later told me, "I had no one and I shut down."

According to my mother, my grandparents refused to answer any of her questions about her biological parents and the adoption, which only left Mom feeling more abandoned. After the death of my grandmother, Mom began a search to discover who she really was and where she had come from. Once again, she had to face another ugly untruth about the secrecy of her birth.

Mom had heard that her birthplace was in Colorado, so she began the journey of searching out a birth certificate. When she was able to locate it, to her dismay, the names of the birth parents shown on the certificate were the names of the parents who had raised her.

Since her mother was now deceased, Mom used the birth certificate to once again confront her father about the adoption. My grandfather had very few words to say about the adoption and, in many ways, his silence allowed Mom to figure it out herself.

According to my mother, my grandmother got pregnant out of wedlock. In an attempt to hide the pregnancy from her family, my grandmother went to Colorado to give birth to my mother. After Mom was born, her parents brought her back to El Paso to live at Wheeler's Children's Cottage, Boarding Home and Day Nursery.

My grandparents then told all of their family that they wanted to adopt a baby who was living at the Children's Cottage. For over three decades they kept the lie alive, until my mother began investigating who her biological parents were. Through all the lies and deception, I think the relationship my mother had with Mother Wheeler was the best thing that ever happened to her as a child. Mother Wheeler gave my mother a sense of self-worth and introduced her to Christianity. Although I found most of the Christian teaching my mother taught me as a child to be harmful to my sense of self-worth, I'm glad she has benefited from her relationship with Christ.

S.T.A.R.S.

El Paso had grown since I had been gone and the drive back from the cemetery took me longer than expected. I followed the only route I knew, which took me back to the east side of town. I stopped by Starbucks, just off Airway, around 12:30 p.m. and ordered a chai tea latte with whipped cream. It's my favorite drink and it always gives me an extra boost when I need it.

I still had an hour before I was to meet Debby, a counselor at S.T.A.R.S., the Sexual Trauma and Assault Response Services. I drove back to the west side of town and around the campus of UTEP—the University of Texas at El Paso—where I was attending college when the Wrestler attacked me. After driving through UTEP, I then drove past my grandparents' home on Galloway Street. I darted in and out of side streets to make sure no one was following me. I was still feeling paranoid. In the back of my mind were the Wrestler's frightening words: "People who tell disappear."

Shortly before 1:30 p.m., I parked my car near the S.T.A.R.S. office. It was located in an old home a few blocks from the Burges House, the place I had moved into after the rape and called home for many years. As I was walking toward the office, I thought back to the first time I called from Minneapolis to report the assault to the El Paso police, and to the various people who had helped me in my attempt to find and confront the Wrestler.

I had made that call because my experience with the Wrestler and the threat that came after led me to believe that he had done the same thing to countless people before and then probably dumped their bodies in the desert. I wanted to find out if there were any unsolved cases of missing young men from the late 1980s and early '90s.

When I called the El Paso Police Department, I sensed that the first officer I spoke to didn't really believe me but he was respectful and took down my report. I thought a detective was going to call me back to investigate further, but a few days passed and I heard from no one. Waking up in cold sweats screaming for help motivated me to stay persistent until someone with authority investigated my report further. Flashbacks of having my clothes ripped off, bite marks breaking my skin open, and gasping for air as the oxygen left my brain were driving me to stand up to this guy.

I called again. The first police officer I spoke to had taken down the information but I was told that there wasn't much he could do for me because there was not a current threat against me. Eventually I was referred to Victim Services, and the person I spoke with there encouraged me to contact Terri Chavira, a detective who patiently listened to my account of what had happened to me in my youth. Once I made the decision to confront the Wrestler, I called Terri and told her I was coming to El Paso. Terri then referred me to S.T.A.R.S., where I spoke with the executive director, Ari Medina. She assigned my case to Debby Gutierrez, a rape crisis counselor.

Debby spoke with me on the phone and then had me sign a release so that she could speak with the counselor I had been working with in Minneapolis. Debby wanted to speak to him before doing anything to make sure I was stable and ready to talk to my perpetrator. I was.

On day two of my return visit to El Paso, Ari was unable to make the premeeting, so I only met with Debby and Liz, another staff member at S.T.A.R.S. Having met with Debby in advance made me feel more comfortable about confronting the Wrestler. I reviewed my impact statement with Debby and Liz and used one of the computers at the S.T.A.R.S. office to clean up a few grammatical errors in my impact statement. Debby then arranged for the confrontation to take place at Family Services of El Paso on Friday, April 7, 2006, at 2:00 p.m.

After my meeting with Debby and Liz, I drove over to the Jane Burges Perrenot Research Center, commonly known as the Burges House.

The Burges House

The Burges House is a grand white home built in the Classical Revival style, with four large columns in the front holding up the roof. It was built in 1912 for Richard Burges, a prominent politician and civic leader of the time. In 1988 it was donated to the El Paso County Historical Society. That same year I was introduced to the Burges House and to the lovely and vivacious Paula.

Paula was a rebel with a certain kind of sex appeal. She was also a mature woman with grandchildren. In many ways she was the polar opposite of what society says a grandmother should look and act like. She was a free spirit with raving reddish hair, long legs, and big breasts that caught the attention of every man she passed. Paula's clothes were bright and colorful, and she wore them like a New York model striding along the catwalk. Her skirts were short, sometimes several inches above her knees, and her jackets fit tight like a bustier on a Victoria's Secret model.

Paula's age would not define her and maintaining her youthful appearance was driven by her desire to live authentically and without the approval of others. Paula and I met by circumstance. One of the local stations featured the Burges House on its news program and encouraged viewers to call the historical society if they were interested in volunteering at the recently donated house.

At the time I was still grieving the death of my father and trying to make sense of my experience with the Wrestler. I remember calling the number on the screen and an older woman answering my call. I told her about the TV report and she was obviously glad to hear from me. She gave me the address of the Burges House and told me when to show up and said I should ask for Dr. and Mrs. Garrett or Paula.

The Burges House is located at 603 West Yandell, a few blocks from downtown El Paso. After parking my car, I remember being in awe of the old house as I began climbing a series of cement steps to the front entry. There were two beveled glass doors leading to an oversized front door. Both were ajar when I arrived for my volunteer duties. After entering the building, I could hear a group of people speaking in a room to the right of the foyer. I was afraid to go any farther, feeling as if I was trespassing. I quietly walked into the room and the chatter came to a halt. The elderly group eyed me with suspicious looks.

"My name is Grant Watkins and I'm here to volunteer. I was told to ask for Paula or Dr. and Mrs. Garrett."

Someone with apparent authority sitting at the end of the

table said, "Welcome. Please have a seat and someone will be with you after our meeting." Apparently I had interrupted their house committee meeting. I sat against the wall and behind the redhead. She looked back at me as if she was bored, smiled, and whispered, "I'm Paula." She then encouraged me to scoot my chair closer to the table where the rest of the committee was meeting. I couldn't help but notice Paula was doodling on the agenda in front of her. She drew pretty flowers cascading down the page and between each item.

It was obvious that she couldn't care less about the points under discussion; she was there to have fun, garden, plant flowers, and, of course, redefine what aging was all about. After the meeting, the committee dispersed and I was formally introduced to Paula and Dr. and Mrs. Garrett. I immediately felt a connection with all of them. Paula took me on a tour of the estate. At first, she thought I was there to apply for the on-site caretaker's position, something I knew nothing about.

The committee had been working on the interior and exterior renovations and had just completed renovating the small one-bedroom guesthouse behind the main house. The entire guesthouse was smaller than my bedroom in my parents' home. Although I was there to volunteer, I expressed interest in the caretaker position and before I knew it, I was moving into the new guesthouse.

The main house was grand and a portion of the second floor had been converted into a small apartment. An attractive attorney had moved in upstairs with her dog and for a while the two of us lived on the estate by ourselves. My mother thought it was great that I was volunteering at the house but early on grew concerned about my safety.

One night as I was enjoying life in my one-bedroom shoebox, I heard a noise outside. I came out of my little house and noticed the gate between the Burges House and the house next door was open. Mr. and Mrs. Webb lived next door and I liked them, although Mr. Webb was a bit cantankerous and didn't approve of the historical society taking up residence next door to his house. Nonetheless, I always did what I could to help look after both properties.

When I went to close the gate, I noticed that the Webbs' back porch window was open and I could hear someone on their back porch. I called out to Mr. and Mrs. Webb, but there was no response. I began peering into the window and was confronted by a man squatting down on the other side of it. He pushed a crowbar toward my face. I was startled and jumped back. *Oh my God, the Webbs are in there and they have no idea a thief is trying to get in their back door.*

I ran back through the gate and then turned back to see the burglar jump out of the window. My hands were shaking so badly that I could barely hold my keys still enough to let myself back into my little house. I was fearful the robber was going to come after me. As my hands trembled, the tumblers inside the lock turned and I made it back inside the guesthouse. I immediately dialed the police and told them what had happened. Within minutes several police officers arrived.

None of us knew if there were more burglars in the house and we were all very concerned about the elderly couple's safety. The house was surrounded by police and eventually Mrs. Webb answered the front door, allowing the police to search her home. The police did not find anyone in the house when they searched it, but they did find a crowbar in between the back door and its frame.

In some ways the attempted burglary drew me closer to Mr. and Mrs. Webb. I really enjoyed getting to know them better, even though Mr. Webb was often screaming and yelling about something. My friendship with Dr. and Mrs. Garrett also grew, as did my relationship with Paula. Paula took a real interest in me and tried to educate me about the finer things in life. We had lunches at the Coronado Country Club and she introduced me to some of her wealthy friends. Paula even managed to get me an interview and eventually a job at Charlotte's Fine Furniture.

I began working at the furniture store in January of 1989 and continued on the job until October of 1992. I really enjoyed my experience there. The job itself wasn't all that great, but it sure beat the work I'd been doing waiting tables at a restaurant named Adolph's Eats & Drinks. At Charlotte's I was selling high-end carpet to very rich people who lived on the west side of town. Rich people would call or come into the store and I would show them carpet samples. It was pretty simple and my closing ratio was high and so was the pay compared to what I had been making waiting tables. Having a decent paycheck and hating to do yard work, I eventually moved out of the caretaker's house. If I recall correctly, I must have moved back in with Mom for a few weeks and then Paula called and told me the upstairs apartment in the Burges House had become available. I moved into it and filled it with fine furniture that I had purchased at Charlotte's.

The El Paso Sun Carnival Association Coronation

In December of 1989, almost a year after starting at Charlotte's, my friend Catherine, who was Coach and Joan's daughter, came home to participate in the El Paso Sun Carnival Association Coronation at the El Paso Convention and Performing Arts Centers. The coronation was held on Thursday, December 21. Catherine was a princess for the Woman's Club of El Paso and I was her escort.

Paula had given me a set of engraved cuff links with my initials on them to wear to the coronation. The night started off great, but I soon found myself feeling out of place and in an awkward position. As I was getting ready to go onstage to greet my princess, I ran into a lady I had met months earlier while waiting tables at Adolph's. I like to call her the black widow. I don't know if it was her unexpected "bite" or her black hair and long arms and legs that reminded me of a spider. What I had come to know about her was that she devoured men sexually like a black widow uses her venom to paralyze her prey before sucking the life out of them.

This lady was volunteering behind the scenes at the coronation, telling the escorts when it was time for them to enter the stage. We were surprised to see each other and our short conversation held me back from entering the stage on time, leaving a gap between when Catherine entered the stage and when I was supposed to meet her.

What made the entire situation so awkward was that I had made a feeble attempt to sleep with this woman at one point. She had invited me to an art show on the west side of town. I think she might have had a crush on the artist and was trying to make him jealous by having me escort her to the art show. Although the woman was several years older than I, I was kind of drawn to her sexually and I was still in a lot of internal conflict about my sexuality. More than anything I still wanted to fall in love with a girl. When we arrived back at her house, we ordered a pizza and then began making out.

While we were making out, one of her old boyfriends rang the doorbell. She then quickly told me I needed to hide in the guest bedroom. I didn't know what was going on and I certainly didn't want to get beaten up, so I followed her down the hall and entered the guest bedroom that was located next to her bedroom. The two of them were having small talk in the front of the house, so I lay down on the twin-size bed and waited eagerly for him to leave the house.

Before I knew it, all the lights were being turned off in the house and I could hear a clunking sound as she and this man walked down the hall toward her bedroom. I must have dozed off for a few minutes but then woke up when I heard flirtatious banter between the two of them. Suddenly I realized I was in some woman's house whom I didn't really know that well and her ex-boyfriend was getting ready to make love to her. This made me really mad and I thought to myself, *I am not going to lie in this room listening to that.*

I quietly got up and entered the dark hallway. The door to her bedroom was only slightly shut, so I peeked in to see what was going on with my date. All I could see was my date lying on her back naked in bed with her legs up in the air. Her ex was making love to her and apparently he had a broken leg, because I remember seeing his cast awkwardly positioned over his backside.

My sense of self-worth was at an all-time low. At the time I must have been twenty-four years old, making moves on a woman in her late thirties, who preferred sleeping with a man with a broken leg. I had seen enough, so I quietly walked down the dark hall and located my shoes next to the front door. I picked up my shoes, went outside, and put them on. It was then that I realized I didn't have a ride to my truck, which was parked several miles away in downtown El Paso.

It was too late to call any of my friends or family for a ride, so I began the long walk home from Sunland Park Drive down Mesa and eventually to downtown. The walk home was horrible. Somewhere along Mesa, I sat down on a bench, only to be startled by a homeless person who was sleeping underneath it. That scared the hell out of me, so I ran across the street and walked in an area that was better lit.

As I got closer to downtown, I walked past a redbrick motel and noticed a lot of cars driving by flashing their lights and slowing down as they approached me. An older man drove by and waved for me to come closer to his car. The old man looked familiar and then I realized that he and his wife came into Adolph's quite often. When I didn't respond to his attempt to flag me down, he moved farther down the street where another young man and some women were standing. I soon realized that these people were prostitutes and they were soliciting sex. Little did I know I was walking through El Paso's red light district, a place I had heard about years earlier from a co-worker when I was working at the Marriott Hotel.

I had worn my dress shoes to the art show and my feet were aching after walking such a long distance. I was glad I only had to walk a few more blocks to my truck.

The following day, still feeling a bit miffed about the entire situation with the black widow, I went over to speak with Mr. Duke at Griggs. When I told him what had happened, he looked at me and asked, "Why the hell would you want to sleep with a woman that much older than you? You need to find yourself a nice girl from church." Behind his look of concern, he did everything he could to contain his laughter. He had a serious but silly grin on his face. Talking to Mr. Duke always made me feel better about myself. He was right. What was I thinking?

Another woman who was organizing the coronation interrupted the flashback I was having and my conversation with the black widow. "You need to get out on the stage and greet your princess."

Once I got out on the stage and greeted Catherine, I looked out into the audience and saw the Wrestler sitting with his wife. They were just a few rows away from the stage. He looked shocked to see me standing next to Catherine. After the coronation we moved across to the banquet hall for dinner. Standing a few tables away from me was the Wrestler with several other young men. When I went to greet him, he moved quickly to the other side of the banquet hall and disappeared into the crowd. What surprises me most of all, as I recall this experience, is that

I didn't feel angry or hateful toward him. I just wondered why he left the room so quickly. Looking back on it, I can see that I had blocked the rape out of my mind but he hadn't and may have been scared that I was going to confront him about it.

More Meetings with the Wrestler

Sometime after the coronation, the Wrestler came into Charlotte's with his young daughter. He was surprised to see me working in the carpet department and quickly appeared uncomfortable. His voice trembled a little when he spoke and he would not make any eye contact. I wasn't feeling uncomfortable and I asked him why he ran away from me at the coronation.

The Wrestler looked surprised. We stepped away from his daughter and he said something about how he had needed to get out of the room because it was a crowded area and he was unsure how I was going to act after what had happened between us. I looked at him a bit confused and then he asked me, "What do you think happened between the two of us?" I told him that he got upset with me because I didn't want to do what he wanted me to do. He looked relieved by my response.

It was as if the rape was hidden from my memory. After all, this was the man who had beaten and raped me, yet that wasn't on my mind at all. All I knew when I was talking to him was that I had done something to piss him off but I really didn't know what.

As we talked in the carpet department, he then told me he was also looking for office furniture and I told him that I could schedule an appointment with someone from the business division of Charlotte's. I explained that we could come out and measure his office space. The Wrestler gave me his business address, which was different from the address I had visited when I first met him a few years earlier. A designer from Charlotte's went out and took measurements of the space, but I don't think much came of their appointment.

After that appointment the Wrestler called me and wanted to know if I would be interested in meeting one of his nephews, who was also coming to terms with his sexuality. I agreed to meet the Wrestler and his nephew at a local restaurant near Charlotte's. When I arrived, I was introduced to a really nice guy and the Wrestler left the two of us to talk and then called me the next day to see what I thought of his nephew. I told him that his nephew was a nice guy but not someone I would consider dating.

The Wrestler then told me about another nephew he had by marriage. He said I should try to get to know him. I don't recall when or where but somehow I met this fellow. He was a nice-looking guy but not someone I was interested in pursuing. I don't recall having much contact with the Wrestler or his nephews after that, but in some ways I still felt captive to the Wrestler. Something had happened between the two of us that was causing me fear and I didn't know what. The Wrestler was something of a powerful businessman and I wanted to gain his approval, yet at the same time I didn't want anything to do with him or his nephews.

Depression

The year 1991 was a difficult one for me. In July my sister and her family moved out of Texas and Mom had begun dating. I spent a lot of time battling depression and trying to find a way to accept myself.

Not having a clear understanding of why I was so depressed, I can recall sitting in my little truck in the parking lot of a shopping mall called Bassett Center telling my friend about the Wrestler. I said that he had beaten me up one night but I didn't call it rape. My friend told me that when he was little, he had been sexually abused by the janitor in his elementary school and he knew how I felt. It wasn't too long after our conversation that all hell broke loose at the Burges House.

El Paso Police Dept. Case 91-214070

On August 2, 1991, around 3:45 a.m., I was awakened by the alarm system. I recall hearing the phone ring and at the same time reaching for the phone to call 911. I was still somewhat asleep and wasn't quite aware of what was happening to me. When I picked up the phone receiver, I remember a person already being on the line from the ADT dispatch center. She called me by name and said there was an alarm alert and wanted to know if I was OK. She then asked if anyone was in the house with me. I told her that I didn't know if anyone had broken into the house or not. Then I heard a noise outside my bedroom door adjacent to the kitchen.

I had been sleeping in the upstairs master bedroom in my king-size waterbed wearing only my underwear. Still foggy from sleep, I tried to sit up several times and then began leaning forward to see if an intruder was really in my house, half losing my balance as I did so.

The operator continued asking me if I was OK and if anyone was with me. At that point a man walked into my bedroom and stood hovering over me in the doorway. It was either a light from the backyard of the house or the moonlight that silhouetted the frame of his body. Backing away from him, I lay back down on my bed and began screaming at him to get out of the house. During this time the ADT dispatch center must have connected me with 911. The person on the other end of the phone kept asking me if I was OK and then asked me to describe the intruder. "He's wearing dark pants, light shirt, and a hat," I exclaimed. I thought he had something in his hand that looked like a crowbar but it could have been something he was trying to take from the house.

As I screamed, my voice began to get weaker and weaker. My mouth became very dry, silencing my voice, and I become paralyzed with fear. The man turned around and exited my bedroom door. I calmed myself down and was able to answer more of the questions over the phone.

"Where are you located in the house?" the operator asked.

"Upstairs in the master bedroom, next to the kitchen and bathroom."

"Do you have a weapon or any guns in the house?"

"No, I don't."

"Officers are outside your house."

I looked out the front window and noticed some sort of sports car in front of the house. Two men dressed in jeans were running up the steps that led to the front of the house, with guns in their hands.

Petrified and screaming back at the 911 operator, I told her there were more intruders out front. She then calmed my nerves by telling me they were undercover cops. Fearing the intruder was still in the house, I thought he might try to hold me hostage if the police tried to corner him, so I ran from my bedroom into an adjacent bathroom and then into the family room located on the second level of the house. From there I made my way onto an interior balcony and opened two French doors that overlooked part of downtown El Paso and Juárez, Mexico.

Standing in my underwear, I was ready to jump off the second-floor balcony into the front yard, when all of a sudden the lights in the family room came on and I saw several uniformed police officers enter it with their guns drawn. I felt a bit scared about the guns but felt more ridiculous standing there in my underwear, waiting to be rescued.

As I was putting on my clothes, the police continued to search the house for any other intruders. After they cleared the house, I was escorted by a police officer down to a police car that was parked in front of the house. In the backseat was the man who had awakened me and tried to burglarize my home.

Apparently an officer who had been dispatched to the house, upon nearing the scene, observed a man walking eastbound on West Rio Grande on the southern sidewalk. Rio Grande runs behind the Burges House. The man matched the description given over the radio, so the officer detained him. The officer then drove the man back to the Burges House, where I identified him. The man was later taken to Central Station and then eventually to the El Paso County Jail.

Sometime after that, a man from the DA's office interviewed me at the Burges House and I later appeared in court to testify against the intruder. After testifying I left the courtroom, so I don't know exactly what happened to him but I heard that he was found guilty and served more time in jail.

El Paso Police Dept. Case 91-318050

A few months later, on November 14, 1991, around 7 a.m. I was getting out of the shower when I heard glass breaking in the lower level of the Burges House. The alarm sounded and the monitoring system called to see if everything was OK. I told the operator I could hear someone downstairs, so the police were sent to the house. I quickly got dressed but stayed upstairs and waited for the police to get there.

Once they arrived I came downstairs and noticed they were detaining a young woman outside the rear of the house. In her hand were a half-eaten apple and a small sample bottle of TECH Stain Remover. The stain remover is a product we used at Charlotte's and often gave away free to customers when they purchased carpet. I must have had one of the samples at the Burges. I suspect the woman thought she was going to get high off that product. The woman was booked in the county jail.

El Paso Police Dept. Case 91-359232

Just over a month had passed when I returned home on December 25, 1991, only to discover I had been burglarized once again. Earlier that evening I had gone out to see the movie *JFK*. When I came home several police cars were parked in front of the house. As I approached, I noticed several people from the El Paso County Historical Society had already responded to the security call from ADT and were standing there with the police. I noticed blood on the window frame adjacent to the front door. Apparently this intruder cut himself trying to enter the house and made quite a bloody mess in the front entry.

After greeting people from the historical society, I began walking up the stairwell to my apartment. A few members of the historical society followed me. After climbing the first few steps to my apartment, I suddenly felt my face turning red as I noticed a box of my condoms sitting on one of the steps. As I looked up the stairwell, I realized there was not just one box of condoms on the stairwell, there were dozens!

I soon found myself, accompanied by a group of curious seniors, stepping over hundreds of condoms. I've never been so humiliated in my life. Once we arrived at the upper landing, condoms were everywhere we looked. I had no idea how I was going to explain this to the members of the El Paso County Historical Society. The seniors did everything they could to keep from laughing as I kicked condoms to the side and made a pathway for us to walk through. They must have thought I was a busy little boy but actually I wasn't. I had opened up a mail-order business called Play It Safe and my intent was to sell the condoms retail via U.S. mail. My business was short-lived because I received a notice from the postmaster telling me that I couldn't sell condoms retail from the PO box I had established weeks earlier.

Just on the other side of a pile of condoms was an officer who told me that once the burglar entered the house, he used a knife to cut the wires on the alarm system. The burglar was found hiding underneath my bed by police dogs as the police were searching the premises.

In less than four months, my home had been broken into three times and my sense of security was shattered. Although I was living in fear, I don't recall wanting to blame the Wrestler for the break-ins. Looking back I think the break-ins were caused in part by a bad decision I had made earlier in the year.

One day when I was leaving Whataburger, a fast-food joint near the college, I had seen a man with a sign that said, "Will work for food."

The man told me he was mentally ill and couldn't hold down a job. I bought him lunch on occasion and he pulled weeds in the yard of the Burges House. One day he arrived with a new sign that said, "Vietnam Vet please help." I asked him if he had been in the military and he said no, but there were other homeless men who had been and he had borrowed the sign from them.

The homeless man started laughing as he told me all the stories he had gotten from his homeless friends and had used to get money from people on the street. "Why work when you can stand on a street corner and make this kind of money?" I realized then that he might be telling his friends that I was living in the Burges House by myself and it would be an easy house to rob. I guess I'll never know for certain who was behind all the burglary attempts.

In October of 1992 I left Charlotte's to work for a furniture store on the other side of town. Although I really liked the owners, working on the sales floor presented some problems for me. The other salespeople were extremely competitive and I didn't feel like I fit in. There were several gay men on the team and I found myself very uncomfortable around them. Perhaps I was hiding from myself.

The working environment was so different from what I had enjoyed at Charlotte's for so many years. I felt harassed by both the straight guys and the gay guys. The straight guys were taunting me about being gay and calling me faggot behind my back while the gay guys were taunting me about not being honest with everyone. They said I was living a double life. One thing I learned is that you can't stand in the middle of the road without getting hit. I soon found myself growing extremely homophobic toward myself and other gay men. I didn't trust anyone and was still living in a state of fear every day from my experiences at the Burges House. Even though it had been almost two years since the last break-in, I was on the verge of a nervous breakdown and growing increasingly suicidal.

In the Hospital

On September 7, 1993, I drove over to Columbia Behavioral Center. It was late at night, after hours, but I knew I needed to get help soon or I'd end up having a nervous breakdown. When I arrived at the center, I told the nurse on duty that I was depressed and could no longer accept the fact that I might be gay. Years of growing up in a religiously conservative home and being raised in a homophobic environment had taken their toll on me. I wanted the so-called gay demon to go away, but it wouldn't. The nurse asked me if I was feeling suicidal. At the time I was not planning my suicide, I was just severely depressed and needed help. Since I was not suicidal and there was no doctor on duty, the nurse asked me to come back in the morning during normal business hours.

The following morning I woke up still feeling depressed and confused. I drove back to the hospital and met with a doctor and told him that if I had to be gay, then I didn't want to live anymore. The doctor admitted me to the hospital and later that day I called my mom to let her know where I was. I remember she broke down and started to cry but then caught herself.

The following day was my twenty-eighth birthday and Captain K called to check in. He was the last person I wanted to hear from. I wanted nothing to do with him or anyone else in my family.

For weeks I slept most of the time and when I wasn't sleeping I was crying and in constant fear of being attacked. Something sinister was bothering me, but I didn't know what it was. I had no idea at the time that it might have anything to do with having been sexually assaulted and almost robbed several times in my home. In my mind, I was only in the hospital because I might be gay. I asked the doctor if I could see a hypnotist to unlock whatever it was that was haunting me or keeping me from accepting and loving myself unconditionally. I knew there was something that had happened to me sexually as a child but was having a hard time remembering what it was. The psychiatrist agreed and I had a few sessions with a hypnotist, but nothing out of the ordinary came up. I felt like I had wasted my time and money.

While I was in the hospital, a young woman in an outpatient program came into one of our group therapy secessions. The type of therapy used in these sessions made use of stuffed animals, dolls, and other things you might find in a theater storeroom. The therapist told the young woman to select a stuffed animal or doll from the pile and to speak to it. Out of nowhere, the doll represented to her a man who had recently raped her. She started screaming at the doll. Her actions took all of us by surprise and then I remember thinking, *Shut the f— up, bitch. I got raped, too, but you don't see me screaming. You need to get tough. Get over it.* Again, I had no idea that my sexual assault by the Wrestler and his friends was affecting me psychologically, and I certainly doubted that a stuffed animal could help me deal with it.

Learning to Love William

Years later, when I was living in Minnesota, I met a holistic doctor who suggested I read a book called *Inner Bonding,* which took a similar therapeutic approach by working with stuffed animals. The book helped me understand that we all have a wounded inner child who needs to be loved. I learned that through calling upon our Higher Power, we can connect with our spiritual self, which can help us be loving toward ourselves and those around us. That loving, adult, spiritual self, when speaking in a loving way to a small stuffed animal or photo that represents our inner child, can help heal the wounds of childhood.

I decided to try connecting with my inner child by carrying on a dialogue with a stuffed teddy bear and a childhood photo of myself next to it in hopes of figuring out why, as an adult, I was in so much pain. At times I felt stupid talking to a stuffed animal and a photo. Yet there was something about the photo of me as a child that captured my attention and helped to unlock the pain hidden deep within my heart.

The name of my inner child was William, which is actually my legal first name. I kept a copy of some of our dialogues in a journal. As you will see, William was not a happy little boy, nor was he a happy teenager or young adult. I never knew what part of my younger life was going to express itself when I tried speaking to my inner child. Sometimes the conversations got a little rough. Yet, despite the sassy and critical comments I sometimes got from my inner child, I knew it was important that my adult self respond with kindness instead of anger. I would call upon my Higher Power for help.

Although, it has been several years since my recovery, I continue to hang on to the teddy bear and photo as reminders of my journey. The following dialogue took place prior to recalling the experience of the Wrestler and his friends raping me.

July 3, 2003, 8:05 a.m.

GRANT: How are you doing this morning?

WILLIAM: Well, it's about time, faggot. What's taken you so long? It's after 8 a.m.

GRANT: I know. How are you today?

WILLIAM: Why do you keep asking me that? We've got work to do.

GRANT: I keep asking that because I care.

WILLIAM: Well, that's a first. You haven't cared for years. Why now?

GRANT: I finally realized what I've done to you. Are you going to be able to forgive me?

WILLIAM: Maybe. Enough of this emotional shit. Let's get to work. We have millions of souls we need to help.

GRANT: OK. But let's go to our Higher Power before we get started.

WILLIAM: Whatever.

GRANT: Higher Power, Love of God, I pray that you will continue to heal the broken heart of our soul and reconcile the difference I have between William and me. He is a loving child. Help me to love him unconditionally. We pray that you will guide us today as we do our work, that we can accomplish a lot and know that we are doing your will. Help us as we go to the website and complete what needs to be done today. Especially the resource page. Guide us as we work out at the gym and watch over us as we feed our body. In the name of our Lord Jesus.

WILLIAM: OK, are you happy? Let's get busy, faggot.

GRANT: OK. I love you.

WILLIAM: F— you.

September 7, 2003

GRANT: Hi, William.

WILLIAM: F— you.

GRANT: What's wrong?

WILLIAM: What do you mean, what's wrong? Where have you been the last few weeks?

GRANT: I'm sorry.

WILLIAM: There you go again, taking off with no regard to me. I hate you, you little f—ing bastard.

GRANT: Is there more to this than me not calling you?

WILLIAM: You said you would play an important role in my life and you don't even call.

GRANT: William, I love you and everything is going to be OK. I promise. Why are you feeling so depressed? How do you feel about Mission for Mobility [a name I gave to my business]?

WILLIAM: I hate it and I hate you, you stupid little fag. It will never work.

GRANT: Why do you think it won't work?

WILLIAM: Nothing works for us because we're stupid.

GRANT: Who told you we're stupid?

WILLIAM: Everyone. We can't even make it in school.

GRANT: You have a college degree.

WILLIAM: The people you date are smarter than us and then they walk away because we're so stupid.

GRANT: Honey, people walk away because they don't like themselves. It has nothing to do with us—me or you. Everyone is working on their own stuff and we can't allow that to affect our self-worth. You are smart and lovable. I love you. How would you like to be in better communication? What can I do to help out?

WILLIAM: You can communicate more with me several times a day and not let people cut us down. Start getting rid of people who hold us back or don't believe in us.

GRANT: Honey, the next time you want to talk, just let me know.

WILLIAM: You'll know. If you are feeling depressed, know that I want to talk.

GRANT: OK. I love you.

I'm not sure what type of therapy I was doing with this dialogue, but as I look back on my life, I realize that after doing it
my life was moving in a more positive direction and I was connecting with this inner child of mine.

I wish I had done more of this type of work while in the hospital, but all I wanted to do there was sleep and hide from the
world.

While I was in the hospital, Joan would come and visit with
me. Many times she would witness to me about the power of
God and the love of Christ. She encouraged me to go to her
Catholic church and get spiritual counseling along with my psychiatric counseling. Joan was confident the church could help
give me structure and comfort during the painful time in my
life. I was eager and somewhat excited about this new opportunity. As a young child, I had attended Mass with my friend
Joey's family. I had developed a preconceived idea that one must
be born Catholic to be Catholic. I had always dreamed about
taking communion and being part of the Catholic Church and I
didn't think they were as mean to gay people as other Christians
were.

After being released from the hospital, I followed Joan's advice and made an appointment with the church office. I was
scheduled to see a priest—I'll call him Padre—to discuss my
feelings of suicide and the need for spiritual guidance. At the
time I was on several medications, including Prozac and sleeping pills. After being out of the hospital for a few days, I started
to feel off balance with the medication I was on, so the doctor
put me back in the hospital for a few days until he could regu-
late the antidepressant. During my second time in the hospital,
Padre came to visit me. For the first time in many years, I began
to feel better about myself. Padre had a profound effect on me
and I began to regain my sense of self-worth. Here was a man in
a position of authority who represented God and told me it was

OK to be myself. The second time I was released from the hospital, I went to see Padre for spiritual guidance. He was new to being a priest and I felt like we had a lot of things in common.

Reflecting back on my time spent at the hospital is also difficult. Very few people know how to respond to mental illness. If you have a physical illness, people usually send you flowers and get-well cards, but if you have a mental illness, people typically do their best to avoid you. I had hardly any contact with my friends and co-workers while I was hospitalized. Many thought I had gone out of town to visit my paternal grandmother in Houston.

I was soon back at work but realized that to stay healthy I would need to give up some of the responsibilities I had. This meant leaving the Burges House and my job caring for the grounds and house. Several friends and my mom helped me move to the Chimneys Apartments on North Mesa. Saying good-bye to the Burges House was difficult because I had to say good-bye to many of the seniors I had met over the previous few years who had served on the house committees and helped me with the upkeep of the property.

It was getting late in the afternoon when I left the Burges House—time to set aside memories and go meet Joan at the Hobby Lobby on Mesa, where we planned to select new silk flowers for the family graves. We picked two different types of silk flowers and assembled the arrangements in the back of the car.

While we were putting the flowers together, Joan invited me to join her at Mass the next morning. I had attended Mass at her church quite often after getting out of the hospital. Now I was reluctant to go back into the church. I was fearful that it would bring back haunting memories of my later experiences with Padre there, including memories of horrible images that haunted me for a long time afterward—images of Christ coming off the cross to sexually attack me. It had taken years of restorative therapy to get over these haunting images.

Therapy had also taught me that if you want to get over something, you must take some sort of action to confront it. Joan and I finished the silk flower arrangements and, on my way back to the east side of town to meet a friend of mine for dinner, I decided that going to Mass would bring closure in many areas of my life. The restaurant where I met my friend was located next to the hotel where I was staying, so after dinner I darted in and out of cars just in case the Wrestler was following me. When the coast was clear, I walked into the Hawthorn Inn and Suites at the El Paso Airport and, after checking to see if anyone was hiding in the closet or under the bed, barricaded myself in the room. I didn't sleep well that night, not sure how I would respond emotionally at Mass in the morning and fearful that the Wrestler would come into my room and take me out before our scheduled meeting at 2:00 p.m. the next day.

CHAPTER FOUR

Day 3

Confrontation Day, Friday, April 7, 2006

When I walked into the church the next morning to join Joan for Mass, I avoided looking at the crucifix hanging near the altar because the crucifix had come to mean something horrible to me. I felt uneasy as I glanced about the pews looking for Padre. In my heart I know it was never Padre's intentions to harm me psychologically, but what happened between the two of us caused me nearly insurmountable pain and anguish. Padre said it never happened, but my memories tell a different story.

Padre's Guidance

Within a few weeks after being released from the hospital, I began to play a more active role at Joan's church. I joined the church choir and started RCIA classes, a program designed to familiarize adult potential converts with the beliefs, practices, and laws of the Roman Catholic faith. I continued to seek spiritual guidance from Padre and also from the monsignor at the church. My conversations with Monsignor remained focused on the love of Christ. The fact that I might be gay was not an issue for him. He continued to remind me that God loves me unconditionally. He also stressed that I must remain celibate until marriage. If it was not God's plan for me to be married, then I had a moral obligation to remain celibate. I would debate with Monsignor about the difficulties of remaining celibate. He continued to remind me that if I would focus on Christ and obey his commandments, Christ would give me the strength to overcome any temptations I might face. I found his insistence on celibacy confusing because Padre was more liberal about sexual activity.

My relationship with Padre got off to a great start. His guidance was easier to follow than Monsignor's; he also always gave me special attention and would often seek me out at church functions. Several times I met him for a beer or bite to eat. Our conversations generally were about gay issues and the difficulties gay people face. Over time, I trusted him more and more and sought his advice on all aspects of my life. Our relationship had changed from spiritual guidance to great friends. At the time, I was in big need of a good friend and strong mentor. In no time at all I had become mesmerized by him.

I constantly complained to Padre about not having a good gay role model. Most of the gay people I know were mean-spirited and I didn't want to be like them and I certainly didn't like being gay. In fact, I hated being gay and I wanted badly to change. I was hoping that by becoming Catholic, somehow my orientation would change. I soon realized that it would not and that I would probably be gay the rest of my life. I thought that if I had a strong role model, then I could find purpose in my life. Padre, who revealed that he was also gay, soon became that role model. I believed in him. I admired the amount of power he had over people, including myself. When Padre shared with me his own sexual orientation issues, I was very excited, because I realized he could truly understand the pain and anguish I was dealing with. Unfortunately, however, the dynamics of our relationship began to change. At this time I was still on medication and under the care of my psychiatrist and therapist. Padre was aware of all this and would often make light of my psychiatric condition. I found these comments painful because I was trying really hard to become a strong person.

I wanted to believe in God and develop a strong faith. Instead I started to believe in Padre and his "doctrine," even though it was contrary to what I was learning in the RCIA classes. My relationship with Padre became more and more intense. He would often pull me out of the RCIA program early so that I could join him for a beer. The RCIA teacher was infuriated by his actions and she cautioned him several times to stop pursuing our relationship, suggesting that it was beginning to cross the appropriate boundaries. I, on the other hand, enjoyed the attention I was receiving from both of them. I began to feel needed and important.

As my relationship with Padre progressed, I began to feel more and more uncomfortable. Our discussion soon centered on sexual issues and Padre's problems with his own personal relationships. I felt sad for him and wished I could offer him some kind of support. However, before long I came to question Padre's motives for telling me about his sexual activity. My initial reaction was sadness, and then it was anger, because I did not believe Padre was staying true to his vow of celibacy.

One night I was visiting with Padre in his apartment when he received a call. The phone call ended abruptly and then Padre began to weep. He was in a lot of turmoil over what appeared to be the end of a friendship that Padre had implied was romantic in nature. I felt sad for him and I wanted to offer him some help, but I didn't know how. Part of me wanted to run. The person I thought was so strong was starting to crack, and so was my foundation. I felt very confused. I didn't want to let go of my friendship with Padre, yet it was undermining my own recovery.

A few days later Padre called me and asked me to meet him at the church rectory. I was still so magnetized by him that I agreed, despite my confusion about our friendship. We met at the rectory and then went to the Surf Club for a beer. My doctors had warned me not to drink while on medication and therefore I just had a soft drink. Padre drank a few beers and then dropped me off behind the church garages. As I was getting out of his car, he playfully groped my crotch. At first I was startled and quickly got out of his car. I then looked at him with disbelief and surprise. *Why did he do that?* I looked at him again and he smiled. I thought for a moment that he was just playing, so I tried to smile back but it felt awkward to smile back. I simply turned away and started to walk toward my car. My eyes soon filled with tears and I remember looking back up at the stained glass windows of the cathedral and seeing a demonic image of Jesus. My mind flashed back to the time when I was young and the boy in the bathroom confronted me and exposed his genitals to me. I wanted to vomit, I wanted to scream, and most of all I wanted to die.

In the following days and weeks, I felt abandoned and my thoughts of suicide increased. I didn't want to turn to Padre for support, but I felt like he had become my foundation. I had found strength in him. I contacted my therapist and told her about my friendship with Padre. I did not tell her about his inappropriate behavior because I didn't want Padre to get in trouble. I tried to downplay the entire event and forget about it. My therapist suggested that I keep my relationship with Padre professional. I would maintain that distance for a few days, but then he would call and I'd agree to meet with him. The dynamics of our relationship had become so intense that I didn't think

I could survive without his direction and yet I didn't have the skills to confront him about what was making me uncomfortable. I didn't have sexual feelings for Padre, but I had become emotionally entranced by his power and felt trapped.

I tried to pray to God for direction and comfort, but my times of prayer eventually became flooded with feelings of horror. Involuntary images of Jesus on a crucifix would arise in my mind that were very frightening. I would see the blood of Christ dripping from his hands and feet onto my face. I could feel the wetness of his blood, only to realize it was the tears from my own eyes. The images of Christ on the cross sometimes turned demonic. The eyes of Jesus would turn red with fire and his ears would become horns. Jesus would gnash out at me and then his face would turn into the face of Padre and then his body would change to resemble that of Padre. The towel that covers Jesus's private parts would soon be ripped off and an erection would appear. This horrifying figure then ripped itself from the cross and chased me. I don't know if the images were induced by medication, my depression, or post-traumatic stress, but they were terrifying.

These images were so strong that I stopped praying to Jesus. I began to feel that I was to blame for what was happening between me and Padre and that I was a demon sent from Satan to tempt Padre.

After a few weeks I began to apply the advice of my therapist and tried to avoid Padre. I met another friend from the church and soon began to date him. I was quite sure this bothered Padre because he soon began to play more head games with me. One day he invited my friend and me to join him for dinner. We did, and he insulted me at the table and told me to leave and go home. I was deeply embarrassed. I excused myself and left. He was acting like a jealous lover and trying to control me. This began a dangerous cycle between the two of us. He would treat me like dirt one day and be nice to me the next. I recall one day he told me in front of a group of people that I was a basket case. I knew I was a basket case and that is why I was trying to get help. Our relationship was much too complex for me and I had no alternative but to quit the church. I simply did not have the communication skills or the self-confidence to confront Padre on these issues. I felt victimized and controlled by him and would not even think about debating anything with him because one minute he would build me up and the next he would knock me down.

Padre would brag about the control he felt when preaching from the pulpit. The power he had over his congregation was incredible and so was the power he had over me. I don't even know if he realized the destructive effect he was having on me emotionally and the profound impact it would have on my life in the years to come.

The Long-Term Effects of Padre

The journey of healing from being hurt by Padre was long and emotionally draining. In some ways the therapy around my experience with Padre was just as dramatic as the therapy I had dealing with the sexual assault and rape. Over the years, the images of Christ coming off the cross evolved into the appearance of blue laser beams coming from his eyes and pinning me down. Therapy brought up a number of issues around religion, spirituality, and God that I had to resolve.

Sometime shortly after I left the church, I spoke to a member of the congregation about concerns I had about Padre based on my experiences with him. One day almost five years later—I believe it was in the late fall of 1999—Joan called and asked me about allegations I had made to the parishioner about Padre. Apparently, the person had come forward and shared my concerns with church officials and they were beginning an investigation. I did indeed imply to the parishioner that Padre had acted inappropriately toward me and that I felt he should not be a priest. I don't recall discussing any specifics of my relationship with Padre and was somewhat surprised that this whole matter had surfaced five years later. I had tried to suppress the entire event in my mind. Unfortunately, since the issue did resurface, I began having flashbacks of the ordeal. Soon I was dealing with insomnia, emotional distress, and an upset stomach.

I also developed severe guilt because some of what I was now talking about with church officials had been told to me privately by Padre. I started feeling fearful that God or Padre would retaliate for my coming forward. At first the church had a priest call me to confirm my story. This priest was very compassionate toward me and therefore I felt compelled to be honest and as direct as possible. I wanted both myself and Padre to heal from our experience, but most important I didn't want any other parishioners to experience what I had.

The El Paso archdiocese flew two members from the church to Minnesota to interview me about my experience with Padre. One was a psychologist and the other was a social worker. Once they arrived in Minnesota, they interviewed me for hours about my relationship with Padre and how it was affecting me. These men were very kind and gracious and I reported to them what I could remember. After they returned to El Paso, they sent me transcripts of the recordings that were made during our interview.

It felt like forever before anyone from the church contacted me again, but eventually I received a letter from the bishop apologizing for my ordeal and offering me assistance in my recovery. I never responded to the bishop's letter, partly because it read as if it were written by his legal advisors. Since I don't think Padre meant to hurt me, and I never had the intention of getting back at Padre or the church for its incompetence, I just did my best to recover on my own.

In the future I intend to write more about my experience with professional victimization, so that religious and professional counselors can learn from what happened to me. I want them to understand how damaging it can be to the people they care for if they cross the appropriate client-counselor professional boundaries.

Ready to End It All

After leaving the parish because of my experience with Padre, I found comfort in my first significant romantic relationship with a man. I had met him at the church. After three years, our relationship came to an end and I was devastated. I moved to Minnesota and a few months later had another nervous breakdown.

My foundation had evaporated. I tried going to a Catholic church in Minnesota, but when I sat down with the priest, I got through about five minutes and then the images of Padre came back. I couldn't call on God to help out. I decided that this was it: I was going to kill myself.

I made an attempt to reach out to my older brother, but the phone call did not go well. He brought up Jesus during the conversation, encouraging me to give my life over to him. Just the mention of the name Jesus triggered dark emotions, and I knew the only way to rid myself of these feelings was to take my life.

I knew committing suicide was going to be hard because my

sister and her husband and small children were a big part of my life and I was living in the basement of their home. The last thing I wanted to do was hurt them or anyone else. But I felt like such a failure. I had gone from living in a big beautiful house to having only two thousand dollars in the bank. I hated the skin I was in, and the emotional, physical, sexual, and spiritual abuse I had experienced had taken its toll.

I took all my savings out of the bank and put it in an envelope for my sister. Then I went to the grocery store and bought a lot of Tylenol and a lot of sleeping pills. I wrote a letter to everybody in my family, explaining that it was just too hard dealing with the fact that I would be gay the rest of my life. I didn't believe there was a God anymore and hoping for change was just too much for me. Then I checked into a local hotel, took all the pills, and waited for them to kick in.

I must have taken at least fifty Tylenol and thirty or forty sleeping pills, all within a thirty-minute period. Everything went black and electrical impulses were shooting off in my brain, almost as if I was watching a lightning show. Then everything got very cold and dark. I kept thinking of myself decaying inside a casket. It was a horrifying experience. Images of my sisters' kids appeared in my mind. The toddlers were reaching up their hands toward me as if they needed me, and I knew I couldn't go through with it.

I tried to stand up and back out of it, but I couldn't get to the phone. I was dizzy and kept falling. I somehow made my way to the bathroom because I felt like I had to pee. Finally I got to the phone. When I picked up the receiver, I couldn't see the numbers. My eyesight had become blurred. I tried calling 911, but I couldn't get the numbers correct and then I just collapsed. Somehow my message got out, though, and the next thing I knew, the sheriff's department was there and I was hooked up to oxygen and taken away in an ambulance.

That was the turning point for me. I promised God that, no matter how difficult things might get, if I were spared, I would dedicate the rest of my life to being of service to others. I thank God for saving me and for not allowing me to have any long-term physical damage. However, it took me a long time to gain an understanding of God that made sense to me. The idea of believing in Jesus as a savior remained difficult. At the same time, I was very afraid that if I denied Christ, I would not go to heaven and I'd spend eternity in hell. Yet when I thought of Jesus, I would have horrific flashbacks of being sexual attacked by him or the image of Padre. A therapist told me I was suffering from PTSD—post-traumatic stress disorder—and suggested that I find another way to think about God.

I needed a God who was not associated with a particular religion or deity. I repeatedly called out to the Holy Spirit for direction. Soon I began understanding that God was not a person in the sense of a human being such as Jesus, but a power much greater than myself that loved me unconditionally. When I sensed that God loved me without limits, I became able to love myself and others in the same way. For me, God is love and there is nothing you have to do to earn that love. I also learned that the way for me to feel God's presence is simply to treat others with love.

The Final Good-bye to Dad

After leaving morning Mass with Joan on Day 3 of my return visit to El Paso, I drove out to the mausoleum to hang the silk flowers she had designed for my father and grandmother. Time spent at the cemetery was short. I hung the flowers and stood in silence before my father's tomb. Any anger or rage I had felt toward him in the past had dissolved and I had found a way to forgive him for not being the father I wanted him to be. I also knew in my heart that my father had forgiven me for not being the son he wanted me to be. I realized again that Dad would be proud of me for standing up for myself and confronting my demons.

I was proud of myself, too, but I still felt nervous that the Wrestler might have followed me to the cemetery. For my own safety I had pretty much decided that after confronting the Wrestler, I would never return to El Paso, and so I was aware that this might be the last time I would ever visit my father's grave. It was time for me to say good-bye to Dad, perhaps forever.

As I drove away from the cemetery, I looked up at the Franklin Mountains. In a weird kind of way, their enormous size provided me a sense of safety. When I was a little boy, I remember watching the world news and hearing about tornadoes that swept through towns, killing many of the people. Dad told me that I never needed to worry about a tornado hurting me because the Franklin Mountains would protect our city and all the people who lived there.

Those mountains remain symbolic for me. Their foundation is strong and can carry the weight of others, their valleys are wide for many to travel, and from their peaks you can see things from a different perspective. In my recovery from sexual assault, a new perspective had evolved. The new vision I had for myself was to help carry the weight of others who had been through similar experiences. My arms would open wide to all those who sought healing and my voice would be used to change the perception many people had of sexual assault.

Searching for Chris and Kent

Feeling powerful, I left the Franklin Mountains and the cemetery and arrived back at the El Paso Airport Hawthorn Inn. It was just past 9:30 a.m. when I checked out. I was ready to confront the Wrestler, but first I wanted to confront the guys who had introduced me to him. What these two guys did to me as a young man was just as vile as, and was a precursor to, the Wrestler's attack. Yet I had not been able to recall any of their actions until I came to acknowledge that the Wrestler actually raped me.

Trying to locate these perpetrators was difficult because I didn't remember either of their last names. Since I couldn't find them through the Internet, I decided to go back to the private school where I first got acquainted with them. This was the two-year college I attended in 1984 shortly after graduating from high school. It offered programs in merchandising, design, and hotel/motel management, and housed a modeling agency.

I hadn't been at the school in more than two decades, but I didn't notice much change outside when I arrived midmorning on Day 3 to confront my past. Months earlier I called the school, asking for the owner or his son to return my call, but I never heard from anyone. I parked in front of the school and pondered for a moment what I would say. When I walked into the school, I was greeted by a young woman. I told her I needed to speak with the owner or his son. Since I did not have an appointment, that request didn't get me very far. The young woman told me that both men were busy. I told her that I was willing to wait. Inside I could see that many things had changed at the school since I attended and it was apparent that they were no longer teaching merchandising and design, nor hotel and motel administration. After standing for a few minutes in the lobby, listening to students and staff, it was obvious to me that the focus of the school was now on technology.

Soon the owner's son came out of the back office. I approached him in the front lobby and asked to speak with him. He was in a rush and said he didn't have time. Apparently, the school was being audited by some agency and he needed to meet someone in the adjacent building. I asked if I could walk with him and he reluctantly said yes. He walked several feet in front of me and appeared to be aloof as I held back my tears and began to share my story:

> *Over twenty years ago I attended your school when your mother was running it. I moved to Minnesota several years ago but now I'm back, trying to make sense of what happened to me as a young man. When I attended your school, one of the guys who worked in the office invited me over to his house and he and his partner took advantage of me sexually. I'm trying to heal from that, and confronting them would help me in my recovery.*

I think he thought I was a nut case, but I didn't care. I needed to find out the full names of these guys and where they were living now.

The man seemed to be growing impatient with me, but he soon realized I wasn't going away until I had more information about the two men. We entered the adjacent building and he asked me to wait in the front lobby while he met with some of his staff. When he finished his meeting, he approached me in the lobby. He appeared irritated that I was still there but was now more willing to listen to my story. As we walked back to his office, I repeated my story and once again asked for his help. He was silent for a few moments and then he told me that the men I was describing to him did not sound familiar to him. I was surprised when he invited me into the office to look through some old school publications. Although I went through several of them from the years I attended the college, I was unsuccessful in finding the first or last names of the men

I was seeking. I handed the owner's son a piece of paper with my name and phone number on it and asked him to call me if he happened to come across any information that might help me in my search. I went away feeling a little defeated, but at the same time I could tell that my sense of self-worth was improving just by taking the steps to stand up for myself.

Dinner with Chris and Kent

That college was where I had met Chris and Kent. Chris worked in the administration office and took an immediate interest in me. Since I was not able to find him listed as part of the staff, I think he must have worked for an employment service and was there on a temporary basis during my enrollment. Chris introduced me to his partner, Kent. Chris and Kent were the first gay couple I had ever met. I had heard about gay people before, but at that time I didn't know any of them personally.

I had often questioned my sexuality while growing up but other than my childhood sexual assault, I had never had a homosexual encounter. I just assumed that being sexually abused as a child, emotionally abandoned by my father, and physically and emotionally abused by my older brother somehow left me broken. I assumed that I would eventually grow out of these feelings and fall in love with a girl and get married.

One night Chris and Kent invited me over for dinner and I was excited about going. Both of them frequently told me how attractive I was and on several occasions Chris implied that he could help get me some modeling jobs with the modeling agency that was run out of the school. I was very gullible.

When I told my mother that I was going to eat dinner at their house, initially she was upset but soon just expressed concern. Mom had her hands full caring for my father and probably didn't give it much thought after I left the house that night. I was still living with my parents during my freshman year in college, and there were few restrictions on my comings and goings, yet I had never pushed the limits by staying out all night.

Chris and Kent were house-sitting for Kent's parents. Apparently his parents were not living in town, and the two guys were watching their home for them. When I arrived, Kent answered the door and escorted me in. Loud music was playing. I think it was either Aretha Franklin or Diana Ross. Kent quickly gave me a tour of the place, and then the two guys asked me if I would like something to drink. I sat at the kitchen table while Chris and Kent were busy making dinner. They made drinks in the blender and then one of them brought a glass over to me. After drinking some of it, I started feeling dizzy and told the guys I was not feeling well. The next thing I knew, the guys were coming over to me asking if I was OK. They asked me if I wanted to lie down and I must have said OK, but on the way to the bedroom I fell down on the floor just outside the kitchen area.

The next thing I remember, as I lay there on the floor, was one of the guys saying, "It's working." Like vultures picking at a dead carcass, the guys began pulling off my clothes.

I didn't know it then, but now I'm convinced the two had given me a date rape drug. I was like roadkill to them and for the next several hours they ate away at me sexually.

I stayed unconscious for most of the assault but extensive therapy has helped me recall waking up during the night needing to urinate and barely being able to move any of my body parts. It was as if my back were glued to the mattress, leaving me paralyzed. Since I was unable to move on my own, Chris and Kent escorted me to the bathroom and held me up on each side as I urinated into the toilet. They then quickly took me back into their bedroom to continue to have their way with me.

To this day it puzzles me that I didn't have any recollection of this experience until I was in my late thirties. Now, on occasion, I still have flashbacks of Chris and Kent twisting and turning my body into a position that would feed their sexual desires. During therapy, sometimes the flashbacks would bring me to my knees, causing me to become extremely suicidal. Memories of the guys successfully stimulating me for long periods of time often cause me the most grief. It was never my intent to become sexually engaged with those two men, and yet for several hours I was enslaved to their sexual whims. My therapist told me that a person who is being sexually assaulted against his will can still be stimulated, especially if he has been drugged.

Sometimes I want to blame myself for the sexual assault, because when I first met Chris and Kent and they disclosed to me that they were gay, I told them that I was confused about my own sexual orientation. I said that because of my religious upbringing I would be too scared to act on any of those thoughts or feelings unless I was drunk or "on" something. The comment was made in passing and I would never have dreamed that they would give me something without my knowledge. Little did I know that I had planted a seed in their minds that would eventually prove to be psychologically devastating to me. Nonetheless, I never instigated sex with them and certainly was unaware they had put something in my drink the night I came over for dinner.

The following morning I woke up in between both men. I had a splitting headache and most of my body, including my genitals, was extremely sore. I remember waking up confused and asking the guys what happened to me. They said I had too much to drink and got a little wild. I remember looking out the bedroom window and seeing my car parked outside. I panicked because I had not told my parents I was staying out all night and thought for sure they would be worried about me. At the time I was only nineteen years old and not yet living on my own.

When I arrived home, Mom had already left for work and Dad was sleeping on the sofa. I don't think Dad was aware that I hadn't come home the night before. When Mom came home from work that day, she did not mention anything about my staying out all night.

I don't recall ever talking about that night with anyone. I just felt dirty inside. When I saw Chris at school after that, nothing was mentioned. I did feel awkward around him but didn't exactly know why. I just didn't want to be around him or Kent. It wasn't long after meeting Kent and Chris that I moved to Baltimore to work at the Marriott.

Hidden Tears

Shortly after I returned to El Paso from Baltimore, I was faced with the shock of walking into my father's bedroom and discovering he had died. I remember crying uncontrollably as I held his lifeless body in my arms. I had lost something I never really had—a dad! Yet despite all the years of sacrifice and anger, in that moment I wanted him back.

Grieving my father's death was one of the most difficult periods of my young adult life. The experience that night in his bedroom was terrifying to me. Frustrated by my attempts to manage my own grief, I sought out the help of a Christian counselor.

What surprised me was the indifference this counselor had toward my dilemma. I was in need of someone who knew how to listen for the messages left unsaid. This counselor made no effort to do that.

As I met with him, I was struggling to find the words that would express my grief. I didn't know what to tell him. I just knew that every part of me hurt. I was holding back the tears. I wanted to cry out, but I couldn't. I never saw my father cry, so I deemed it wrong for me to cry. I hid the tears, crying deep within myself. Crying on the inside caused me further grief. I remember staring into the therapist's eyes, thinking to myself, *You stupid f—ing bastard. Can't you hear me?* I needed this therapist to dig deeper. I needed him to hear my cry, but he couldn't because he wasn't listening to me in the first place.

Sometimes I would look up and he would be yawning. Once he was even yawning as he handed me a tissue. At times he would be glancing down at his watch. He simply hadn't developed the skill to communicate in a caring way. I often think of the times I wanted to shake him until he would connect with my reality. He didn't get it.

What made matters worse was that the therapist was a retired Baptist preacher. I viewed him as an authoritative person representing the faith I had been raised in. This faith had taught me that being homosexual is a sin and that God hates sin, so I thought God must hate me since I was born that way. That meant I should also hate myself.

When I went to see this therapist, I was overwhelmed by the complicated and sometimes conflicting mix of needs and beliefs I had. I knew I needed to find some resolution to my grief. I also knew I wanted to be a Christian and to be straight. I think in the back of my mind I had hopes that this Christian counselor could help me change my sexual orientation. At the same time, I had an opposite desire—to gain approval from the Christian community, to hear from someone who would say that it's OK to be you, that we love you and accept you just the way you are.

I couldn't find a way to express any of this adequately to the therapist, and he did nothing to draw it out of me. Whatever I said to him was met with indifference and an unspoken attitude of judgment. I was sure that his responses were based, in part, on the fact that I had disclosed my sexual orientation to him. I think he wrote me off after that, blocking the healing process that needed to take place. I have always recalled these sessions with the pastor-therapist as a waste of time and money. I had not found any of the help I was seeking, and the judgment and lack of interest I felt from him made it even harder for me to accept myself. I had allowed the therapist's belief system to block out the discovery and acceptance of my own beliefs. At the same time I realize now that he was probably doing the best he could, based upon his own life experience and the point of view he probably held about what caused a person to be gay. I have wondered if, after all the years of counseling young Christians, he ever came to the realization that nothing anyone does causes a person to be gay. The person is just born that way.

Many times I walked away from these therapy sessions feeling angry. I received absolutely nothing from them. In fact, I think I suffered from his inability to hear my cry—a cry that was kept inside me for several more years after that horrific night of being sexually assaulted and after finding my father dead in his bed. If I had been heard and accepted in those earlier years, I believe I could have begun the healing process much more quickly.

I should have been seeing a grief counselor or even a traditional counselor, not a Christian family counselor. A traditional counselor would have put aside any personal religious theology and helped me learn to accept myself.

Eventually I did find a different therapist who had the skill of listening without judgment. This time I felt safe and was able to share how I was feeling. I was also able to listen and hear the hard questions she was asking me; for example, "Have you ever been sexually abused or assaulted?" Such promptings made me think about the obvious. She helped me find the courage to answer questions that had to be addressed if I were ever going to recover. She created a safe place where I no longer needed to hide my tears. I no longer saw myself as the victim of my experience but rather as a reflection of it.

Introduction to the Wrester

Not long after my dad died, I decided it was time to move on from working at Griggs. Joan lined up an interview for me at Adolph's, a local hamburger joint, where I could make good tips and work fewer hours than at Griggs. I don't know if Mr. Duke was ready for me to quit or not, but I don't recall him suggesting that I stay. I moved on to Adolph's but still picked up shifts at Griggs every once in a while.

At Adolph's I waited tables and struggled to fit in socially with the straight guys. I lived in fear of most of the heterosexual young men my age, especially if they were athletic and masculine. These guys reminded me of my brother and the other kids I grew up with who bullied me. Many of the Hispanic male staff members saw me as an outsider, not only because I was Anglo, but also because they were extremely homophobic. One day as I left work I saw that someone from the restaurant had written "faggot" all over my Ford truck. The cooks, many of them younger than I was, would often prepare other people's orders before mine. One of the bartenders often did the same. The result was that some of the customers I was serving got angry with me because people who came in after they did were being served before them. In addition to having to put up with this kind of treatment from the staff, I was embarrassed about still waiting tables in my early twenties, so I was eager to find a way out of there.

One night while I was waiting tables, Chris and Kent came into the restaurant with the Wrestler. This was the first time I had ever met the prominent El Paso businessman. It had been several years since I had seen Chris and Kent, and I did not think about what had happened before with them. I don't recall being angry at them or uncomfortable with the fact that they were in the restaurant. All three men took a strong interest in me and talked about how good-looking I was.

Feeling like a failure and not having a strong direction for my future, I basked in the attention I was getting from them. The guys suggested that I begin modeling, and Chris and Kent offered to take photos of me. The Wrestler told me he had connections and could help me launch a modeling career. There was talk about branding my image and private labeling merchandise after me. All this attention was very exciting for me, and I began seeing myself as more than just a waiter. I began to dream again, and over the following couple of weeks I trusted these guys to make me into something more than what I was.

Soon I had scheduled an appointment with Chris and Kent for photos. I went out to their home, which was different from the one where I had dinner with them on the night of their sexual attack. The guys had pulled out several outfits for me to try on. Some of the clothing was formal and some casual. After they took photos of me, they soon asked me to try on a robe for a more seductive look. I followed their lead because I felt like they were the experts.

After I tried on the robe, they asked me to take off my shirt and just wear shorts. They said they would need a variety of photos to be able to market me. After they took photos of me in my shorts, Chris suggested I take off my shorts. It was at this point that I felt something sinister lurking behind all their kindness and got this horrible feeling. I felt dirty and I didn't want to be next to Chris or Kent. Chris made some sexual reference, and with that I excused myself and went home. Although I now have images in my memory of their sexual attack on me, at the time I didn't. Sometime after the photo session, the guys came back to the restaurant to give me copies of the photos. I was pretty excited about becoming an international model and was certainly eager to see the photos but didn't want much to do with Kent and Chris. There was something I didn't trust about them, but I didn't know what it was.

That night I showed the photos to Barbara, one of the waitresses on staff. She was not amused and thought the photos of me in the robe and shorts were too seductive. I dismissed her comments as insensitive and childish. Barbara and I got along well, but she wasn't on great terms with several of the other waitresses, so I thought she was just trying to get even with me because I was friendly with most of the female servers. I now see that she was looking out for me, and I should have paid attention to her concerns.

An Invitation from the Wrestler

The relationship Kent and Chris had with the Wrestler struck me as a bit odd because a straight guy doesn't usually hang out with two gay guys. Then one night the Wrestler came into the restaurant near closing time. He sat in one of the booths by himself and I asked him what brought him in so late. He said, "You do." Initially I wasn't sure if the Wrestler was coming on to me or just trying to be a mentor. In hindsight I guess he was setting up the attack that would happen later.

Having very few strong male role models, I liked the attention I was getting from him, but I knew that I was not interested in having a sexual relationship with him. At the time, the Wrestler struck me as being old, ugly, and fat. His nose was shaped awkwardly, resembling that of a bulldog and when he grinned, his teeth hung out like fangs on a werewolf. Yet, at the same time, his sense of confidence about himself was very attractive. He asked me if I wanted to join him for a drink after my shift that night, but I was tired and eager to go home. Although he looked disappointed, he gave me his business card and told me to give him a call.

Sometime later I did phone him and he asked if I would like to join him for a drink after work. I agreed to meet him late that afternoon at his office, which was just a few blocks from my parents' home. When I arrived I walked into the reception area, where I was greeted by a secretary. I asked for the Wrestler by his last name and mispronounced it. The secretary laughed hysterically. The Wrestler has a Spanish last name and I pronounced the vowels in English instead of Spanish. It was a little embarrassing, but the secretary told me not to worry about it after she pronounced it correctly for me. She then called the Wrestler and told him I was in the front lobby waiting for him. After she hung up the phone, she pointed me in the direction of his office and I walked back to greet him.

When I entered the Wrestler's office, he got up to greet me with that familiar artificial grin of his. Suddenly he pushed me a few times. At first I thought he was being playful, but then he did it again. This time he repositioned himself in front of me, blocking the office door I had just come through. I don't think I even responded to his odd behavior. Years of conditioning from being beaten up as a kid by my older brother had taught me to just keep quiet and take it.

The receptionist who had greeted me couldn't hear any of what was going on because she was quite a distance away from where we were and I hadn't seen any other staff as I made my way back to the Wrestler's office. Within just a few minutes of being pushed, I soon found myself pinned up against the back wall of his office. He began rubbing up against me and his fangs looked like he was about to take a bite out of my face. I tried pushing him off, but he wasn't budging. I turned my face to the left, looking out his office window. There appeared to be a grocery or some sort of retail store with people coming and going. I thought about crying out for help, but I didn't think anyone would hear me through the glass. To my right there was a door leading to a common area hall and I could hear someone moving about. Suddenly the Wrestler let go of me and started to make small talk about the photos Chris and Kent took of me. I was certainly shaken by the experience, but I really didn't know what to make of it. Was I reading too much into it?

The Wrestler and I then walked out of his office complex and he again told me how much he wanted to help me succeed. I'm not sure if I understood what had just happened to me because of my history of being abused and my low self-worth; I couldn't think clearly about the situation. I responded to him as if nothing was the matter and said OK when he asked me about getting together again. I don't recall getting a bite to eat or a drink that afternoon, and I realize now that his invitation to dinner was just bait to get me to come to his office.

⁊

It wasn't too long after my visit with the Wrestler that I got a strange call at my parents' home from a young man claiming to have seductive photos of me. I asked him where he got the pictures and he said he got them from the Wrestler and that the photos were being distributed all over town. The caller identified himself as the Wrestler's lover. This didn't make any sense to me because the Wrestler was married.

The young man wanted to know if I was romantically involved with the Wrestler. I told him that I wasn't and that the Wrestler was only trying to help me launch a modeling career.

I told the guy that those photos belonged to me and I wanted to pick them up. I think this guy was eager to meet me in person, so he invited me out to his home on the east side of town. I arrived at a single-story townhome and the Wrestler's lover, who looked younger than I, came outside as I pulled up. I think he was just as confused as I was. He offered to give me my photos back if I would stay away from his lover. I assured him that I was just friends with the Wrestler and didn't want anything to do with him sexually or romantically.

It was obvious that this guy was a kept man and I felt sorry for him. He was frail looking, almost anorexic. His self-esteem must have been lower than mine and I could tell he was certainly under the spell of the Wrestler. He told me that the house he was living in was owned by the Wrestler. On my way back to my parents', I felt angry that the photos of me were being distributed all over town without my permission.

When I got back home I showed the pictures to my mother and told her what had happened. She went ballistic and although I was not nude in any of the photos, many of them were too provocative for her. Mom ranted for at least a good hour about the people I was hanging out with. She suggested that I destroy all the pictures and stop hanging out with those fellows. I dismissed my mother's behavior as overprotective and ignored what she was telling me.

I then called the Wrestler to ask him what the hell was up with this feminine guy who had my photos. The Wrestler was embarrassed and told me the he would handle the young man. He said I shouldn't worry about him calling me anymore. As for the photos, the Wrestler told me he had pictures of lots of young men in his desk drawer and wasn't sure why I was so upset. I told the Wrestler that I wanted all my photos back and he told me I could come and get them at his office. When I arrived, the Wrestler handed over what remaining photos he had of me and told me not to be so upset. He started coaching me about business and he invited me to go with him on a sales call to two of his retail customers.

I'm not sure if the Wrester was the president or a vice president of the company he worked for, but I felt like it was an honor to be around someone so successful. On the way over to the first retailer the Wrestler told me that he was married but working on a divorce and, yes, the guy I met was his young lover. I asked him how his wife felt about all of this and he gave the impression that at times she got upset over it but for the most part she enjoyed the lifestyle. The Wrestler said he could provide for her and the kids. The woman he had married was also a working professional and probably could have raised and supported the children without the Wrestler's income. Why she stayed in the marriage I do not know. The Wrestler often talked out of both sides of his mouth; sometimes he said they were separated and other times he talked about a pending divorce. Whenever I asked how his wife was doing, it made him uncomfortable. I don't think the Wrestler was ever separated or filing for divorce from this woman. He needed her in his life so that people would not discover he was a sociopath who liked to rape young men.

After leaving the first retailer, the Wrestler told me that the young lover often traveled with the family and on business trips. The young man was petite and very flamboyant and was wearing makeup the day I met him. I asked the Wrestler how he explained the lover to his business associates. The Wrestler told me something I have never forgotten: "I tell them he is my nephew. People never expect the obvious."

The Wrestler was great at giving advice. I was ready to hear anything he wanted to say and share with him all of my struggles. I was still grieving the death of my father and feeling like I had no direction in my life. We often talked about my father and I recall the Wrestler telling me that he played sports for my father when he was in high school. Today I don't think he ever did know my father; he just said he knew him to gain my trust. The guy was a habitual liar, but I was too naive to see it.

His visits to the restaurant were becoming more frequent, and many times his wife and kids would come with him. On one occasion he and his wife came in with another couple from their church. His wife always seemed uncomfortable around me. I was always friendly to her and just assumed that she was struggling with the possibility of a divorce. I also assumed that she knew that I knew their secret and she was fearful of being exposed.

I admired the Wrestler, and although I've never been sexually attracted to him, in my attempt to gain his fatherly attention I think I may have led him on sexually. I certainly didn't do it on a conscious level, but as an adult looking back I can see how that might have happened. Initially, the Wrestler was always making sexual innuendos, but since he had a wife and a lover to meet those needs, I just didn't take any of them seriously. I wish I had followed my mother's advice and stayed away from him.

Since I had made myself clear to him that I was looking for mentoring and coaching, it was not uncommon for me to meet with him for some professional advice. Sometimes we would meet at a place called Bombay Bicycle Club, not far from Bassett Center.

The last invitation I got to meet him for a drink was near my birthday. The Wrestler called and I remember telling him that I was celebrating a birthday and he offered to buy me a drink at Pelican's Restaurant. I still get choked up thinking about what happened to me that night.

Confronting the Wrestler

On Day 3 of my return visit to El Paso, after handing over my business card to the owner of the school where I had first met Chris and Kent, I drove over to Chico's Tacos and munched down on a high school lunch tradition of rolled tacos in simmering mild hot sauce topped off with cheese. I then drove across the street to the Kmart and called my mom, who had moved to another state several years after my father's death. I had not told her I was traveling back to El Paso for fear she would want to come with me. I just didn't know how safe things were going to be and didn't want anyone to get injured in case things didn't go well. Mom remained strong on the phone, as she always does, but I know she was very concerned about my safety. After hanging up I called Mrs. Duke to tell her that I was in town and how sorry I was about the death of Mr. Duke. Mrs. Duke was grateful for my call and it felt like I had some closure with my time at Griggs Restaurant.

I still had some time before my 2 p.m. meeting and I didn't want to be open prey sitting in the parking lot of Kmart, so I drove up to Scenic Drive and to a viewing station on the side of the Franklin Mountains. I didn't recall it being so isolated until I arrived and parked my car. As I began to reflect, I stayed in my car for safety reasons and looked down from the mountainside at the city I called home for so many years.

Suddenly I heard a thump on the door next to me and my heart began to race. This was it, I thought. The Wrestler was about to take me out before I could confront him in front of others. As I began to block my face with my hands from a would-be assassin, a woman motioned with her hands to say she was sorry for tripping and then falling against my car. I took a deep sigh and got out of there.

My heart continued to race as I made my way to the Family

Services of El Paso building. Many thoughts were going through my mind, and I was afraid that the Wrestler was not going to show up. When I arrived at the building, I entered a side entrance and was met by Debby, the rape crisis counselor. I thought for sure that I would be greeted by police and the detective who had taken my call over the phone, but there were no police, just Debby and me. I asked Debby if the police were coming, but she said only if we needed them. I had thought that maybe undercover police might be hanging out in the lobby and parking lot. I wanted so badly for this man to be exposed for who he was.

Debby informed me that the Wrestler was already waiting for me with her boss in the conference room. There was no court order making him appear, because of the amount of time that had passed since the actual rape. I don't think the police ever talked to him about it. As I entered the conference room, I could see the Wrestler sitting on one side of the table facing Debby's boss. To my surprise he looked relatively good for a man his age. He was still extremely overweight but also appeared to be muscular. He was well groomed and dressed in a light-colored shirt with a tie and business slacks. All I could think was, "People never expect the obvious" and *who in the world is going to believe that this married man rapes young men?*

I was well prepared to meet with the rapist. Prior to leaving Minnesota, I met with a rabbi whom I had got to know through a social circle of mine and asked him if he was willing to meet with me to review the letter I'd written—my impact statement. I got the sense that even the rabbi was uncomfortable talking about the issue of rape or maybe he had heard that I was a nut case struggling with the sexual assault issue and just didn't know how to respond to me. Nonetheless, he had made the following great suggestions: *Stay in control. Read slowly. Take time to pause. Watch your tone and overall body language.* The rabbi then suggested I let the Wrestler know that there was nothing legally I could do against him and that I was not trying to ruin him professionally. He said I should tell him, "The only thing I can do is forgive you, but you would need to ask for forgiveness." I know asking for forgiveness and being forgiven can be powerful for the healing process, but I don't recall bringing the subject of forgiveness up at our meeting and know for certain the Wrestler didn't ask for forgiveness. All he did was sit there with his head down making notes in his BlackBerry. He never made eye contact. He just sat there like a guilty, pathetic fool.

The conference table was large and the Wrestler was sitting directly opposite me, several feet away. Debby and her boss sat at the end of the table separating the two of us. Debby began the meeting by thanking us for coming and then turned to me to begin. I too thanked the Wrestler for coming and told him that I was not out to destroy him but out to recover from what he did to me and also help others to recover. I took a deep breath and, in my authoritative voice, began reading the letter.

April 2006
It has been almost twenty years since you savagely raped me and I wonder if you ever think about it. I still do. Do you ever wake up in cold sweats screaming for help? I do. Do you ever have nightmares of someone chasing you and holding you against your will? I do. Do you ever think about what it's like to be held down and choked? I do. Do you know what it's like to gasp for air as you feel the oxygen leave your brain? I do. Do you know what it feels like to have a man twice your age and size beat you up? I do. Do you know what its like to have your clothes torn off of you? I do. Do you know what it's like to be forced into sexual acts against your will? I do. Do you know what it's like to have someone bite you with all his might, breaking your skin open? I do. Do you know

what it's like to have a penis forced into your rectum, ripping it open and leaving you to bleed?

I do.

Do you know what it's like to hate yourself so much because you have been raped and because you lacked the confidence and strength to defend yourself? I do. Do you know what it's like to have your young adult life stolen from you? I do. Do you remember the night you raped me? I do. It was the night you took my dignity, self-confidence, and self-worth away. It was the night you almost broke my spirit.

I've often wondered if you ever felt guilty about your attack on me, but I was too afraid to confront you. I remember your threats the day after you raped me and your successful attempts to make me feel guilty. If I recall correctly, you told me that I deserved it and that I was a whore. At the time I didn't understand why you would call me a whore because my sexual experiences were extremely limited, at least the ones I was conscious of. It wasn't until the last few years in therapy that I came to fully realize how you and your friends set me up. This letter only addresses you, the rapist, and your evil and horrific sexual assault on me.

If you can't remember exactly what you did to me, I will remind you. I met you shortly after my father's death and my 22nd birthday at a restaurant where I was waiting tables. You took a special interest in me, and over the course of time I shared with you my sadness and immense pain of losing my father. You told me that you played sports for my father back in the early '60s and how much you admired him. You pretended to be a friend of my father and I began to trust you. In some ways you filled a void for me and I confided in you about my lack of self-confidence and struggles in life. As our friendship developed I began to trust you. If you recall, my father had been very sick for several years and I was under a tremendous amount of stress in caring for him. You told me that you could help launch a modeling career for me and also offered to take me hunting, fishing and to sports games. You said you missed out on having a son and these were things of interest to you. These were all things that were very important to me because my father's illness had prevented me from doing them along with him.

On one occasion I told you I needed to buy a car and you offered to help me select a used one. When we went to look for the car you told me that you would buy me a car if I were willing to be involved with you romantically. I told you that was not what I was looking for, and our friendship ended for a while. You then stopped in to the restaurant with your wife and kids and acted as if had I misunderstood you. Once again I began to trust in you and found comfort in your emotional strength and wisdom.

Over that year I continued to grieve the death of my father and I confided in you that I had been molested as a child and was confused about my sexual orientation. You shared with me that you struggled with your own sexual orientation issues. One night you called to ask if I would like to join you for a drink. I agreed to join you, and while at the restaurant I complained to you that I had to sleep on the sofa because my grandparents were in town. You told me that you could get me a comp room at the Westin Hotel. I accepted your offer to take the room and said that I was willing to talk more about our lives. When we arrived at the Westin Hotel, it was sold out and you told me not to worry because you also had connections at the hotel up the street. When we arrived at the hotel, I became very nervous and uncomfortable about the situation and did not want to enter the hotel room with you. After several minutes of hesitation, I entered the hotel room. You became very quiet and looked at me demonically.

Realizing I had made a horrible mistake, I told you that I wanted to leave. As I began to turn around, you hit me on the right side of the head and used your left arm to put me in a headlock. *You put a chokehold on my neck and began to unbutton my shirt and pants. You took your foot, pulled down my jeans from behind, and forced me on to the bed. We struggled for a while and I fought for my life but eventually you succeeded in ripping my clothes off. You forced me on my back while hitting me several times across the face. I continued to scream and you began to choke me. You eventually turned me over and piled pillows on top of me, preventing my cry for help from being heard. You held my hands above my head and wrapped the sheets around my head and then began to penetrate me. The pain was so extreme I felt like someone had taken a knife and was stabbing me in the rectum. As I continued to scream, you continued to bite, hit, and choke me. Eventually I stopped moving and you pulled the pillows and blankets from my head to see if I was breathing. At that time I hit you in the face with my head, broke away from your hold, and made it to the bathroom. I locked the door and laid on the bathroom floor bleeding. You knocked on the bathroom door, at which time your personality changed once again, and you began to apologize for your behavior. I screamed at you and you left the hotel.*

The following day you called me and asked if I was OK and wanted to know why I over-reacted. I told you that you had hurt me and that I had hundreds of bruises and bite marks all over my body. You told me that I was now your sex slave and the marks should serve as a reminder to me. I told you that I was going to tell, and you told me that people who tell disappear. You told me that no one would believe me because you were a pillar of the community and nobody would expect the obvious. You said you would destroy me if I ever told. Little did I know that I was destroying myself by remaining quiet.

Your attack on me left me wounded but not destroyed. It impacted my ability to trust others socially and has prevented me from sustaining long-term romantic relationships. It slowly chewed away at my self-image and prevented me from reaching my fullest potential academically and professionally. There have been times when the impact your assault has had on me emotionally and physically has been unbearable and brought me to my knees spiritually.

Perhaps this was the greatest lesson I learned from my experience with you. If we surrender to a higher power when we are in our greatest pain, we will be greeted with a caring soul who offers a place of healing and recovery. I have been blessed with a supportive family and friends who carried the burden of my pain when it was too difficult to carry myself. They offered me the presence of love, which created an opportunity for me to heal. For that I'm forever grateful and will repay them by advocating for others.

You are a very sick, demonic man and need to get help for your illness. I have become empowered despite your evil attempt to destroy me and with the grace of God have found the strength to move on with my life, and have transformed the pain, hurt, and anguish into a healing ministry that will help others who have been wounded. What I want of you, now twenty years later, is for you to spend the rest of your life coming to terms with all the people you have exploited physically, financially, emotionally, and sexually. Please realize and accept responsibility for the fact that your self-centered actions have robbed others of their happiness and inner peace—and for some, their lives.

Survivor—Grant Watkins

After I finished reading my letter, the room was silent. Then Debby said something like, "This concludes today's meeting and I want to thank both of you for coming." Again, a short moment of silence filled the room and then the Wrestler said, "I need a few minutes" as he typed on his BlackBerry.

After he said that, I stood up and spewed out all the anger and rage I had felt for all those years directly toward him. I yelled, "You are not in control of this meeting. I am." The Wrestler started to stand up and I could see his hands were shaking. He quickly sat back down. I let him know that he had robbed me of many years of my life and that if he ever tried hurting me, my family, or my friends, I would expose him for the rapist he was. I know I also threw in a few cuss words but I don't recall what they were. I then concluded the meeting.

After the meeting I waited in one of the counselors' offices until Debby and her boss escorted the Wrestler out of the building. At first the Wrestler drove away but then came back and waited outside for me. Debby's boss went outside and motioned him to move on. Debby came into the office and congratulated me on a job well done. She had nothing but praise for me and I felt young and free again. I asked Debby what the Wrestler said when I left the room. She reported that the rapist said I had him confused with someone else. There are a lot of things in life I've been confused about, but being raped by the Wrestler is not one of them.

I left the center that day feeling good about my progress and was grateful that I had the opportunity to express myself to the Wrestler. Debby's boss told me about a shortcut out of the building that I could take just in case the Wrestler was still waiting for me. I drove around town for a while and then met up with Joey's parents, Joe and Juanita, for dinner. Since I had been on the phone most of the day, my battery was low and I was unable to retrieve the calls from Debby checking to make sure I was still OK later that afternoon. Apparently everyone back at the center was quite concerned about my well-being. Finally when my phone was charged, I called Debby and let her know that I was OK.

After a wonderful dinner, I checked in at the El Paso Radisson Suite Hotel under my assumed name of Mr. William Le Dale and had one of the most peaceful nights of sleep I've ever had.

CHAPTER FIVE

Day 4

Leaving El Paso, Saturday, April 8, 2006

Before leaving El Paso on Day 4, I went to pick up an old neighbor whom I grew up calling Aunt Betty so that we could have breakfast together. I recall the day she moved into the house across the street from us. Aunt Betty tells the story like this.

"My moving day was not going well. The June heat was oppressive. My throat was dry as dust. The movers had just dropped a treasured antique lamp in the driveway. I picked up the pieces and fought back my sadness.

"I looked up from the ground to the sound of ice in a cold pitcher of lemonade that was near my face. The pitcher was in the hands of a young man who looked down at me. 'Would you like some cold lemonade, ma'am?'

"I gratefully gulped that frosty lemonade as I eyed a young man about twelve years old, skinny as a bone, with a sunburned nose and tousled hair. He said, 'I live across the street.'

"That was the beginning of a friendship between Grant and me that has lasted the years. I was 'Aunt Betty' and we shared secrets over snacks in my kitchen quite often.

"One day Grant came to see me with troubled eyes. We settled at the kitchen table for fruit juice with guacamole and chips.

"He confided in me that he was not the best of students. He was afraid of what the future would hold for him as a grown-up.

"I told him, 'Good manners and honesty open doors of opportunity.' I told him that if he did his very best in school and was always courteous and honest, then he would not have to worry about his future."

Aunt Betty was older than my parents but younger than my grandparents. She had blond hair and big blue eyes. What I really liked about Aunt Betty was her open-mindedness and her mentoring nature toward me. She was the first vegetarian I had ever met. I recall one day driving over to Wendy's with her to get some lunch. Aunt Betty ordered a baked potato and I ordered a combo meal with a medium Coke and fries. I remember that Aunt Betty changed my Coke order to ice water and we skipped the fries. Once I got my burger, Aunt Betty encouraged me to throw away the meat inside.

I don't recall if I actually tossed the meat or just hid it from her, but I know I felt a little cheated over losing my Coke and fries. While in middle school, I spent some of my summertime sweeping the floors and handing out flyers at Aunt Betty's vitamin store, which was located in downtown El Paso.

Sometimes when Aunt Betty got home from work, I would bring over homework assignments and Aunt Betty would play the role of study buddy. One day my social studies teacher gave the class an assignment to interview a neighbor about what impact the environment has on our culture. I successfully talked Aunt Betty into completing the entire written portion of my so-

cial studies assignment. Although I was conducting the interview, I had her write down the answers. Each time I verbally
asked her a question, she would look at me with her big blue
eyes and say, "I think you're supposed to be filling these questions out, not me." But I insisted that the interviewer was only to
ask the questions and the person responsible for answering the
questions was also responsible for completing the written portion of the homework assignment.

Since the project was about how the environment affects our
culture, somehow Aunt Betty talked me into carrying a rosebush to school the following day. It was in a container that
would dissolve once placed in the ground, thus avoiding adding
a plastic container to our landfill. The school was several blocks
away from my house. It seemed that I got poked by a nasty thorn
every step of the way, and it was embarrassing to arrive at school
with an overgrown rosebush in my hand. I guess that was my
payback for trying to get someone else to do my homework.

Aunt Betty was among the first people I ever told about being
confused about my sexual orientation and she was extremely
supportive. Since I was also suffering from low self-esteem,
Aunt Betty invited me into her home office one night to listen to
a subliminal recording. As I lay on her daybed, Aunt Betty read
personalized wellness affirmations into a recorder. I think there
was soft music playing in the background on the recording in
addition to Aunt Betty's voice. After my session was over, Aunt
Betty handed me the tape and told me to listen to it every day
until I started feeling better about myself.

Before we left her place to go to breakfast, Aunt Betty filled a
small box with a few personal items she wanted me to have
to remember her by. Inside the box was a small statue of what

appeared to be an American Indian woman, a mirror the size of a serving dish, and an iron kettle that looked like it belonged on a covered wagon. After placing the box in my car, we drove over to a truck stop just off Airway to eat huevos rancheros.

It was heartwarming to eat at the restaurant because I reflected back on the times I had eaten there as a child with my family. Aunt Betty appeared to be frustrated with me for not contacting her when I first arrived in El Paso, but I told her that I had been concerned about my safety and didn't want to place her in any danger should the Wrestler or someone he knows be following me.

Aunt Betty, now in her late eighties, teared up as I shared my story with her. After we left the truck stop, Aunt Betty insisted on having the items she had given me wrapped and boxed up so they wouldn't get broken on the flight back to Minnesota. We stopped by a local retailer who ships and packages items. Packing everything was labor intensive for the clerk, and I felt guilty when Aunt Betty pulled out her credit card to pay for the services. I offered to pay, but I think Aunt Betty knew my trip to El Paso had set me back quite a bit with the cost of airfare, hotel, food, and car rental expenses.

Aunt Betty had moved from the house across the street from my parents, and I think this made saying good-bye a little bit easier. We drove around for a while before I dropped her off, just to make sure no one else was following us and she would be safe. As we said our good-byes, I realized how blessed I was to have grown up next to her and the importance of having long-term friendships.

Leaving El Paso

After my visit with Aunt Betty, I returned the rental car and walked into what I considered the free zone. Standing amidst airport surveillance cameras and security guards made me feel safe again. The Wrestler would be stupid to try anything now. As I walked through the metal detectors, an inspector pulled me to the side and wanted to see what was in Aunt Betty's care package. For a moment I thought that maybe the Wrestler knew someone with Homeland Security and I was going to be redirected out the back of the airport to an unmarked car.

I was relieved when all he wanted to do was to cut open Aunt Betty's package. I soon found myself frustrated when the box was opened up and all the plastic popcorn chips came tumbling out over the countertop and onto the floor. It was nearly impossible to repack the items as securely as they were packed originally. Still I was very thankful to have cleared the metal detectors and to be on my way back home. Breathing another sigh of relief, I made my way to my departure gate.

Behind a crowd of people was a window from which I could see the Franklin Mountains. I walked up to the glass to get a better look. The glorious mountains reminded me of the courage it took for me to confront the Wrestler. That confrontation was my way of protecting the young men of El Paso from the Wrestler. Did he ever stop raping men after he raped me almost two decades ago? Would my act of confronting him and bringing it to the attention of the authorities make him think twice before raping again? I prayed that it would.

Back Home

Once I arrived home, family, friends, and co-workers continued to express their overwhelming support. I thought for sure the nightmares and paranoia I had felt prior to confronting the Wrestler were finally over. I soon discovered that is not how recovery works. Sometimes I had good days and then all of a sudden I would be hit with an unexpected flashback of the attack.

I became increasingly fearful of being by myself, thinking that maybe the Wrestler was going to travel to Minnesota and try to kill me here. His haunting words, "People who tell disappear," played over and over in my mind.

I often had the fantasy that undercover detectives would catch him right before he had a chance to rape a young male. Or they'd find him in some sort of inappropriate conduct with a minor. Then he would finally be arrested and the citizens of El Paso would all be safe.

For weeks after I returned home, I found myself checking the *El Paso Times* online every day to see if the Wrester had been arrested. Instead, I found business-related articles about him. One of the articles put him in contact with more El Paso youth. Another article talked about him being in a position of authority with young high school graduates. My heart ached and I found myself crying almost every day for fear that he might be raping these young people.

I reached out to one of my past allies in El Paso, asking for her support if I decided to go public with my story; but after leaving two messages, I realized she had grown tired of my emotional rants and was not going to return my calls. I phoned the detective I was working with in El Paso and left several messages for her to contact me about what I was reading about the Wrestler in the *El Paso Times*. It was sometime later that the detective called me back. She explained that the cell number I was calling no longer belonged to her, and that my calls had been sitting dormant in voice mail until the phone was reassigned and a new detective retrieved my messages. I was told again that there was nothing the police or legal system could do for me. I had waited too long to report the incident and it was my word against his.

By the time I heard back from the detective, I had already grown tired of hating the Wrestler. I was also further along in therapy and no longer felt the need to fight the battle in El Paso. Gradually I was coming to accept the outcome and realizing that my justice was the day I confronted him in front of two El Paso health care professionals.

Telling My Story

I continued in therapy for a short time and eventually stopped having nightmares. I was having very few flashbacks. I turned my energy toward helping other survivors in Minnesota and became a frequent speaker for a program of the Minnesota Department of Corrections called Minnesota Circles of Support and Accountability (MNCOSA).

MNCOSA volunteers help high-risk sex offenders successfully reintegrate into society. The first time I shared my story I could hardly get through the presentation without getting teary-eyed. However, the more I shared my story, the more I realized that it no longer had control over me and I was using my energy in a more productive manner. As I got more and more comfortable sharing my story, I began to meet other men who had also been survivors of sexual abuse, either as children or young adults.

There are two responses I often get when sharing my story with other men. The first is they don't want to hear about it—they try to cut me off. I often wonder if these men were also survivors of sexual abuse and the conversation was too difficult for them. Or maybe they were perpetrators and what I was sharing with them caused them to be overcome with guilt.

The second type of response I get from men is initial shock but then engagement. One time I told my story in front of a

Toastmasters group and one of the members got up abruptly when I had finished and left the room. I thought he must be homophobic and the topic was taboo for him. The person conducting the meeting called for a short break so that people who were evaluating my presentation could finish up their assessments.

Suddenly the man came back into the room and extended his hand to me. He told me that male sexual assault is very common in his home country of India and the culture there doesn't allow anyone to discuss it openly. He praised me for sharing my story and encouraged me to keep talking about it so others could begin the healing process. What he found most amazing about my story was my humanity—my unwillingness to retaliate against the Wrestler with physical violence and the amount of time I was spending trying to reduce occurrences of reoffending by supporting work done at the Department of Corrections. Having him acknowledge this meant a lot to me and inspired me to continue writing my story so that I could share it with the rest of the world.

CHAPTER SIX

Turning Point: Going Public

The moment we begin to fear the opinions of others and hesitate to tell the truth that is in us, and from motives of policy are silent when we should speak, the divine floods of light and life no longer flow into our souls.

Elizabeth Cady Stanton

In April of 2009, three years after confronting the Wrestler, I was asked to speak in El Paso at S.T.A.R.S.'s Twelfth Annual Border Issues Conference on Sexual Assault. S.T.A.R.S. invited me to deliver a keynote speech on a book I had written during my recovery titled *CPR for Caregivers: Connect, Project, & Reflect through Mind, Body, and Spirit.* After my address, I was given the opportunity to share my personal recovery story at a breakout session. I had come far in my recovery over the past few years, and I was now ready to speak out to the citizens of El Paso. To me, sharing my story publicly meant that I was now whole again and in a position to help others.

The night before my presentation, I had dinner with Ari and Debby from S.T.A.R.S. Ari had been the first person at S.T.A.R.S. to hear my story when I first called there, and Debby had been my counselor. I had never met Ari before, but she was exactly how I would have imagined her—a fighter, courageous and willing to have difficult conversations in order to create social change. Although I had met Debby before, I had never seen her sense of humor. She has the ability to light up a room and lift one's spirit. Her spirited demeanor was exactly what I needed and I was grateful to experience her wit.

The day of my presentation I had breakfast with Terri, the detective I was referred to when I first called the El Paso Police Department and reported my sexual assault. She had spent hours listening to me on the phone and I felt that she believed me from the very beginning when others did not. I had never met Terri in person prior to having breakfast with her before my presentation. The tone of Terri's voice during our phone calls was always soft and gentle, yet conveyed a sense of self-confidence. I expected her to be very pretty, but I had no idea that she was going to be an absolute knockout. Had she taken another career path, she could have easily become a New York model.

Little did I know until I met her that Detective Terri worked in a part of the police department that handles calls from—well, let's just say people who aren't very stable. Apparently not very many people at the police department believed what I was telling them, so I was connected to her department.

I'm not angry at anyone for not believing me, because whenever I spoke to someone at the El Paso Police Department, I was always treated with dignity and respect. I suppose if I were an officer there and I received a call from some man who was having an emotional breakdown over something that happened to him almost two decades earlier, I too might question the authenticity of his story. At the time I was telling this story to the police, much of it was still buried in my memory and I was confused about the sequence of events.

During our breakfast together Terri gave me a card that read:

Grant, your courage and unselfishness have helped and will continue to help so many! I thank you for showing me that carrying a gun does not mean you're courageous; standing up for others and yourself and what is right is truly courageous. God bless.

Her kind words reaffirmed that no matter what scrutiny I received from others, I have made the correct decision by coming forward and sharing my story.

After breakfast I returned to my room and changed into a suit to deliver my keynote and personal story of recovery. I was feeling a little apprehensive but not overcome with fear. I knew what I would share was the truth and it needed to be told. My friends told me that for the first few minutes of the keynote I sounded a little nervous but soon had the attention of the entire room. After the keynote address, participants were given the option of attending various breakout sessions. To my surprise most of the participants stayed to hear me share my painful story.

My opening words were, "Sometimes I don't want to tell my story anymore, but when I think about *not* telling it, I feel the grip of the rapist choking me all over again. I don't want other boys and men to suffer like me."

The room remained quiet as I told participants about the day I called my perpetrator, asking him to meet with me. I then read aloud my impact statement and followed up with the events that had taken place after the confrontation. I ended by lighting a candle and reading a poem I had written:

Face the Hate After the Rape

Secrets to speak, yet scared to tell
Voicing hate for him would only destroy
I stayed silent, self-hating instead

At last it came time
To face my hate, break silence, escape
Tell my true Texas story, male sexual rape

Met a man, his wife, young kids
Some called Uncle, a mentoring guy
A deceiver of young, with money a tease

While I grieved Dad's death, this wrestler attacked
Nightmares remind me, memories reflect still
These sexual acts against my free will

Torn off clothes, naked slave to same-sex plea
Pinned, choking, gasping, hands held down
Broken skin, bleeding, penetration begins

Lacking strength and confidence to defend
Self-worth and dignity stripped away
Broken of spirit, the haunting begins

Years of hiding, hating, shame
Sanity shattered, time to move far away
Where a therapist asks, have you ever been raped?

———————

Hidden memories revealed, self-worth restored
I call and tell my hometown cops
In search of my abuser, I want to set things straight

Still living, I wondered, hurting young men like me?
Google finds him, this business VIP
This straight man who rapes men

———————

His eyes on his BlackBerry, silent he sat
Yet he *had* to hear, to face what he'd done
To apologize. *Did he ever stop?*

As I spoke, strong and confident now
He listened, unmoved, yet the truth was told
At last unpinned, freedom is mine

———————

It happened to me, did it happen to you?
Spilling the secret is the key
Leave the silence, use your voice to break free

The ignorant will tell you, you deserved the abuse
Leaving you powerless to get up and move
Communication is power, speak your truth

They call you liar, crazy, confused
You're blamed and feel dirty, yet you're not at fault
The abuser is the one who is confused and unclean

> Anger and rage could seal your fate
> Instead use your story to liberate
> From your heart, communicate, don't retaliate
>
> People care. You won't be alone,
> Ears listen, hearts hear, millions pray for you,
> The Holy Spirit can guide you through the storm
>
> Your emotional hurt will eventually end
> If you do the work to reveal what's within
> One day you'll feel whole again

When I had finished, participants stood up and applauded. Their applause told me they trusted, accepted, and respected me. A bond had been established, and I felt young and free again.

After my presentation I grabbed some lunch and headed to the airport feeling pretty good about bringing male sexual assault awareness to the El Paso area. Then I passed a small gift store at the airport. On the front page of the *El Paso Times* was an article about the conference, but nowhere did the article mention anything about male sexual assault.

I immediately had feelings of despair as I sank deep into a chair that was facing a window overlooking the airport runway and the Franklin Mountains. My happiness had turned to immense sorrow, and for a few minutes I felt like I had wasted my time returning home to El Paso to share my story. No one cares, I thought. I could feel the Wrestler's hand once again choking me. I gasped for air, not realizing that I was so upset I was unconsciously holding my breath.

My inner voice of fear was quick to point out that the rapist had won again. *He must have threatened the media with something. That's why no one else is coming forward to talk about this topic. Everyone is scared of him, including the media.*

Then I realized that overall the conference was well covered by the media and I reminded myself of the coverage my story did get. Diana Washington Valdez, a writer for the *El Paso Times,* did bring attention to my story in an article published on the Friday before the convention, and a man from the city's ABC affiliate, Channel 7, had interviewed me for a few minutes the day before the event. Yet, to my knowledge, nothing else was reported about it.

I couldn't help but wonder how the citizens of El Paso were ever going to prevent male sexual abuse if they didn't know it was happening. The media had the opportunity to tell my story in great detail, but they chose not to. How is anyone going to heal if the situation is not exposed? Looking back up at the Franklin Mountains I realized that, even though the media didn't hear me, more than 150 people had heard my story that day and that was more people than I had ever told before.

Unpinning myself meant becoming self-responsible and coming to terms with who I was and that meant learning to love myself unconditionally by connecting to my own mind, body, and spirit. This connection gave me the courage to accept myself and speak out against the abuse.

Who I Have Become

When I began the recovery process, it took a tremendous amount of courage to face my fears. Every part of me, both physically and emotionally, hurt. I often felt nauseous, alone, and misunderstood. At the time, I wasn't looking for some sort of personal transformation; I just wanted God to take away the pain.

Karol, the therapist I was seeing, asked me to write down

an affirmation and to read it whenever I was feeling fearful, including when I was afraid to do what was necessary for my recovery. The affirmation soon became a mantra for me in times of trouble: *I will not let my fear keep me from moving forward.* Although facing my fears took immense courage, my doing so made the emotional and physical pain go away. Every area of my life transformed and a new self-image evolved.

Recovery did not take place overnight. It was a process, with an "aha" moment every once in a while. At each stage I discovered that I was much more than my experiences. The recovery process chipped away at the inauthentic parts of myself and I rediscovered my spirit, the invisible force that drives my life today. My recovery has led me to live a different kind a life, one of service, friendship, and faith.

The first thing I began to notice after facing my fears was an internal desire to live a life of service. Things I valued in the past, such as appearances, wealth, and the need to feel powerful, just weren't important to me anymore. I don't consider it wrong if other people value these things; I just don't spend a lot of time thinking about them anymore. My joy comes from seeing the human spirit alive in others and encouraging them to move past self-imposed physical and mental limitations to achieving greater levels of success in their lives.

At first, I initially worked at providing affordable housing to seniors and people with special needs. Eventually I expanded my reach by engaging thousands of volunteers in helping to support affordable housing in their own communities. Living a life of service has made me realize that I am living out my purpose here on earth.

The second transformation I noticed during my recovery was a change in many of my relationships. At the time of my epiphany, many of the people in my life didn't understand sexual abuse and the impact it has on the people who survive it, nor did they really care. Some people told me to snap out of it or to just get strong. If it were only that easy! Some friends silently faded away from me and started rumors that I was a freak, crazy, or an emotional time bomb ready to go off. I can remember seeing some of these people in public, whispering to the person they were with and then walking away, pretending they had not seen me at all. As much as it hurt, I'm glad I got to experience that. It taught me to love others despite the difficult times they may be going through. It also reminded me of my own ignorance as a youth, when I expressed similar behavior.

What was amazing to me were the new people who came into my life and offered me the support and love I needed to recover. At the same time, my recovery was leading me to a certain level of maturity and a realization that I needed to leave some people behind who were not growing in the same direction I was. I walked away from them because staying connected was too painful. It kept me in a state of despair. Losing these friends didn't make me sad, though, for I know we all have lessons to learn and experiences to encounter that draw us closer to discovering our own spirit. Some of these friendships were eventually renewed. Celebrating the reconciliation of a friendship gone bad is the ultimate expression of joy that I have felt here on earth. Over time, trust begins to form again and a mutual understanding of unconditional love begins.

The third transformation I noticed was developing a new kind of belief in God and a spiritual path that supports me. Today, I no longer live in fear of God or have a particular image of what God does or doesn't look like. I don't feel a need to be saved or to follow a particular religion, and the old ideas of God that were causing me so much misery have been replaced with unconditional love for myself. I no longer ask God to forgive me but rather to give me the strength to go directly to the people I feel I have wronged and ask them for forgiveness. I do believe in an afterlife where I will be accountable for my deeds, not the creed I proclaimed while on earth.

I have respect for my Christian friends, and I also embrace and respect people who are not Christian. I think some religions aren't open to criticism and use the notion of sin to control their members. I would rather fill my heart, mind, and body with gratitude, forgiveness, and ultimately unconditional love than adhere to any doctrine that has a history of brutality and domination.

My faith in the Holy Spirit is strong. It may not be the same faith that others proclaim, but it's centered in love and service to others and it's in alignment with what I believe God wants from all of his creation. I've learned that some people don't like it when they see something that is different or is not in agreement with what they believe to be true. Since I no longer have the fear of what others think of me, I have experienced a newfound freedom.

"People never expect the obvious." That is what the Wrestler told me in my youth. He used fear to intimidate me and keep me from expecting the obvious. Fearing what others may think of me, I could no longer distinguish for myself what the obvious was. Even years later, the cause for much of the physical and emotion pain I was going through should have been obvious. Yet it took a lot of courage and a lot of help to learn to read these clues and heal what hurt. I still experience moments of fear sometimes, but that fear no longer controls me when I realize that it's been days, if not weeks, since I've had any flashbacks. I suppose there will always be a faint memory of the past, but those experiences don't define who I am, and when they do, I boldly say out loud, *I will not let my fear keep me from moving forward.* In that moment, the divine floods of light and life flow into my soul and I realize I am spirit.

Afterword

After confronting the Wrestler, I reflected back on the friends and caregivers who stood by me and those who abandoned me early on. I thought about what caregiving for another takes, especially the enormous strain my mother experienced as she cared for my father. I thought about the countless caregivers I had met professionally who took care of people living with chronic physical and mental disabilities.

My reflections on these experiences inspired the book *CPR for Caregivers: Connect, Project, & Reflect through Mind, Body, and Spirit.* Initially, I wrote that book to help keep other caregivers from burning out, but after I completed it, I came to realize that the principles I shared in it were also ones that I was using to care for myself and were instrumental in my recovery. They are principles of self-renewal. I highly recommend anyone recovering from illness or caring for someone with an illness to read that book and be inspired by the simple process it describes. You can also find more information about the three-step process for self-renewal on my Web site, www.grantwatkins.com.

Whether you are caring for yourself or for someone else, know that one day the journey will come to an end and the old you will disappear. The experience itself will have stripped away all that's unimportant and what will be left is the real you.

May you love unconditionally,
Grant Watkins

Information about Sexual Abuse and Assault

The following three sections, "Male Survivors," "Myths and Facts," and "The Impact of Sexual Abuse and Assault," are reprinted, with permission, from the Web site of

Neighborhood Involvement Program
2431 Hennepin Avenue South
Minneapolis, MN 55405

Male Survivors

Boys/men don't cry.

Suck it up.

Boys will be boys.

Don't be a sissy.

Take it like a man.

These are all phrases commonly heard today that mold the expectations for boys and men to be brave and strong. In our culture, men are not supposed to be victims of any kind, least of all, of sexual assault and abuse. Society labels these men as less manly for "allowing" themselves to be victimized. These pressures make it difficult for men to speak out when something is wrong and consequently, many men continue to suffer in silence.

Men sometimes mask their fear, sadness, grief, and pain behind a tough exterior.

Many males experiment sexually in a variety of ways during childhood and adolescence. While some of this may be developmentally appropriate and nothing to be concerned about, the tendency to view all sexual experiences, except the blatantly obvious ones, as harmless is the result of social learning that prevents boys and men form recognizing what hurts them. "Boys will be boys" leads to "men will be men" and perpetuates the belief that these are normal behaviors without harmful consequences.

Myths and Facts

MYTH: Only women can be sexually assaulted.

FACT: Men can be and are sexually assaulted every day and their perpetrators can be male or female.

MYTH: Men who sexually assault other men are gay.

FACT: Sexual assault is not about sexual orientation or desire— it is an act of power and control. The motivation of the perpetrator is to humiliate and/or brutalize another person.

MYTH: Male childhood survivors of sexual abuse or assault will become perpetrators.

FACT: While many perpetrators were themselves victimized, the majority of survivors do not continue the cycle of violence.

MYTH: Men assaulted by other men must be gay.

FACT: Both straight and gay men can be raped; most studies report that at least half (and more often the clear majority) of victims are heterosexual.

The Impact of Sexual Abuse and Assault

Trust
Establishing and maintaining relationships may be difficult. Many problems can be traced to difficulty being vulnerable and trusting others, including oneself.

Compulsive Behavior
Most compulsive behaviors serve the purpose of alleviating anxiety and avoiding pain. Frequently seen compulsive behaviors include sex, alcohol and other drugs, work, gambling, exercise, and food.

Sexuality
Confusion may arise in male survivors around sexual thoughts, desires, and behaviors. Letting go of unhealthy or compulsive sexual behaviors is possible. Sorting out one's sexual orientation on the straight/bi/gay continuum can be challenging. Reclaiming a healthy sexuality is possible when a survivor is ready.

Physical Symptoms
Physical symptoms are not uncommon. Some areas of the body may be extremely sensitive to touch and there may be a general tightness or tension within the body. Frequent headaches and other body aches, hypertension, and sleeplessness are not unusual. Sometimes the rectum can be injured from forced anal penetration. Sometimes there is a feeling of being disconnected from one's body like it belongs to someone else.

Feelings and Thoughts
A variety of feelings and thoughts may be associated with sexual assault. Some of these include depression, rage, anxiety, hopelessness, shame and guilt, thoughts of suicide, difficulty concentrating, memory problems, and flashbacks.

Resources

*For more information about Grant Watkins,
please visit www.grantwatkins.com.*

Study Guides for Groups

Study guides are available at www.grantwatkins.com for group
use in discussing and understanding the issues raised about
sexual abuse and assault in *Unpinned*.

Minnesota Resources

Breaking Free
www.breakingfree.net

Council on Crime and Justice
www.crimeandjustice.org

Comunidades Latinas Unidas En Servicio (CLUES)
http://www.clues.org

Hennepin County—Sexual Violence Center
www.sexualviolencecenter.org

Men's Action Network
www.menaspeacemakers.org/programs/mnman

Minnesota Coalition Against Sexual Assault (statewide referrals)
www.mncasa.org

Minnesota Indian Women's Sexual Assault Coalition
www.miwsac.org

Minnesota Office of Justice Programs
www.dps.state.mn.us/OJP

NARAL Pro-Choice Minnesota
http://www.prochoiceminnesota.org

Neighborhood Involvement Program
(Rape and Sexual Assault Center)
www.neighborhoodinvolve.org

Outfront Minnesota
www.outfrontmn.org

Planned Parenthood
www.ppmns.org

Prevent Child Abuse MN
www.pcamn.org/index.php

Ramsey County Sexual Offense Services
www.co.ramsey.mn.us/ph/yas/sos.htm

Sexual Abuse Prevention Network
www.survivorsnetworkmn.org

University of Minnesota—
The Aurora Center for Advocacy and Education
www1.umn.edu/aurora

Other Resources

Depression Symptoms
http://www.rsac-nip.org

National Center for Victims of Crime
www.ncvc.org

National Sexual Violence Resource Center
www.nsvrc.org

Rape, Abuse and Incest National Network
www.rainn.org

Sexual Assault Nurse Examiner (SANE)
and Sexual Assault Response Team (SART)
www.sane-sart.com

Sexual Trauma and Assault Response Services (S.T.A.R.S.)
www.stars-elpaso.org

Stop It Now!
www.stopitnow.com

Victim Rights Law Center
www.victimrights.org

About the Author

Grant Watkins writes and speaks nationally on caregiver burn-out and sexual assault awareness and prevention. Grant is the author of *CPR for Caregivers: Connect, Project, & Reflect through Mind, Body, and Spirit*, a guide that helps professional and personal caregivers achieve life balance and self-renewal. *Unpinned: Breaking the Hold of Sexual Assault and Abuse*, is his most passionate work yet. Grant's interests are leading with what he calls "spirit" and sharing his gifts through community engagement and volunteerism. He has spent most of his professional life in service to others by advocating for affordable housing for low-income seniors and people with chronic physical and mental challenges. Grant has a bachelor's degree in communication and lives in Minneapolis, Minnesota.

For more information about Grant Watkins, please visit www.grantwatkins.com.